Law of Attraction

The Basics Of Manifestation Secrets To Attract Anything You Desire

(Hacking The Law Of Attraction For Money For Satisfaction And Success)

Andrew Gordon

© Copyright 2022

Published By **Andrew Zen**

Andrew Gordon

All Rights Reserved

Law Of Attraction: The Basics Of Manifestation Secrets To Attract Anything You Desire (Hacking The Law Of Attraction For Money For Satisfaction And Success)

ISBN 978-1-77485-459-4

All rights reserved. No part of this guidebook shall be reproduced in any form without permission in writing from the publisher except in the case of brief quotations embodied in critical articles or reviews.

Legal & Disclaimer

The information contained in this ebook is not designed to replace or take the place of any form of medicine or professional medical advice. The information in this ebook has been provided for educational & entertainment purposes only.

The information contained in this book has been compiled from sources deemed reliable, and it is accurate to the best of the Author's knowledge; however, the Author cannot guarantee its accuracy and validity and cannot be held liable for any errors or omissions. Changes are periodically made to this book. You must consult your doctor or get professional medical advice before using any of the suggested remedies, techniques, or information in this book.

Upon using the information contained in this book, you agree to hold harmless the Author from and against any damages, costs, and expenses, including any legal fees potentially resulting from the application of any of the information provided by this guide. This disclaimer applies to any damages or injury caused by the use and application, whether directly or indirectly, of any advice or information presented, whether for breach of contract, tort, negligence, personal injury, criminal intent, or under any other cause of action.

You agree to accept all risks of using the information presented inside this book. You need to consult a professional medical practitioner in order to ensure you are both able and healthy enough to participate in this program.

Table of Contents

Chapter 1: You can unlock the power of your desire .. 1

Chapter 2: The Importance Self-Love 13

Chapter 3: Analyzing your current situation and the gap between your current circumstances and your goal 32

Chapter 4: The Role of Vibration as well as belief systems in the Law of Attraction 36

Chapter 5: What you can do to apply the Law of Attraction to find love 47

Chapter 6: LoA and Personal Growth 53

Chapter 7: Making sense of affirmations 61

Chapter 8: DETERMINING and UTILIZING A GROWTH MINDSET 70

Chapter 9: Ways to Make Universe Work for You Using the Law of Attraction 96

Chapter 10: Visual Thinking: Step by Step instructions for Programming Your Mind to make more money, gain power and Respect 107

Chapter 11: Power of Mindfulness Meditation 123

Chapter 12: What to Make Use of LOA to manifest various things 142

Chapter 13: Law of Attraction Exercises 151

Chapter 14: Top Law of Attraction Myths debunked 161

Chapter 15: Health Attraction Mantra 175

Chapter 16: Master Key System 181

Chapter 1: You can unlock the power of your desire

What if I said that attraction laws are at work in your life?

It's possible to think that I'm a complete idiot. You're reading this book to find out why. There are some things that don't go well in your life, and you're in need of a solution. What makes anyone think it's the law of attraction working for you?

In reality that things happened as they did because of the things you think about.

Based on what you're focusing on

This is what is the basis of law of attraction, which states that you will attract the reality you constantly pay attention to.

We're not talking about things you claim you'd like to have and wish for and aspire to; nor am I speaking of things that others claim you must work for or would like to have. Instead I'm talking about your daily life.

Do you think about the extent to which an enslaved person you are? Do you take your time thinking about choices that you believe were mistakes made in the past and why things have gotten so bad due to these decisions? Do you have people in your life or in your past who you are unable to accept? Do you have a type of a ready-made excuse to explain what causes things to go wrong?

If one of these applies to you, then the laws of attraction are operating within your life. Because wherever your attention is the emotional, psychological and spiritual energy flow.

Have you noticed how much you think about your issues the more complicated they appear to become and the more out of your control?

It's not an incident. It's the way you do, which is why you're living the way you're living.

The positive side? the law of attraction could help you the same way it can work against you.

If you're or are in any way dissatisfied with the way you're experiencing, take note of this. It is possible to turn things around. Here's how to put the law of attraction to work in your favor.

Do not ignore your desire's power

Begin to envision the future you would like to see. Sounds easy, doesn't it?

The issue is that many people carry various beliefs from their past. Some religions are more guilty than other denominations. It's still a long-running practice in many religions to deter the desire to be wealthy. Indeed, some claim that wealth is bad or even a red flag.

If you were raised in a similar setting, it should not be a shock to you to discover that in your heart you are feeling that the desire for something more isn't good.

As harmful as the religious aversion to science is scientific dogma.

Perhaps you were raised in a non-religious home and your parents taught you in your brain that imagining things in reality is unwise and foolish. Perhaps your parents quickly dismissed this as non-scientific and not grounded in the reality. It's just as depressing as the dogmas of religion.

You might not be aware of the potential to desire within your life due to the fact that you are unable to distinguish it from wishful thinking. Perhaps you think that hoping and wishing for something is equivalent to wanting it.

You're in a state of confusion; it's not surprising the fact that you're energy also dispersed. It's not going exactly where it's supposed be The law of attraction does not work for you.

The desire is often lost in the midst of other emotions

Sometimes, from time moment, you show genuine desire. It is a flash that fades and disappears from the world. If it does, it's extremely bright, intense, and very illuminating.

However, it won't take long before it fades out and then revert to a blur. It is replaced by other feelings, or even a kind confusion in the mind. This is because people experience a variety of emotions every day. It's not necessary for me to explain what this happens.

If you're in the middle of something and it

appears like it's in your mind, this clarity quickly gives way to anxiety about how to pay the rent or any issues in your personal relationships. Perhaps, the mental impression of your employer pops up to mind and you feel angry and helpless or confused.

There are so many thoughts running through your head. And every one of them can trigger feelings which can impede your moments of clarity, especially when it comes to your desire.

In this light It's not surprising that it's easy to lose your focus. Welcoming to our club. The majority of people experience this which is the reason the majority of people lead lives without guidance.

Every now and then an emotion of joy ishes over you and things begin to become more clear. However, these moments are only temporary since "the remaining of your existence" gets in the way.

In the event that you talk to the majority of people and ask "are your living the lifestyle you've always envisioned?" the vast majority will reply, "no."

The sad truth is that the majority of us live the lives we're supposed to live. That's right. We have earned our existence by the way that we have, as well as the decisions that flow from these thoughts. We're entitled to this.

It's a tough pill for lots of people to swallow because life isn't easy. It seems like a lot of the events that went badly in people's lives are caused or triggered by circumstances and people that were not under their control. Who can say they are not responsible for their circumstances?

I'll direct your attention to a nagging reality: forces and other people outside your control can be the ultimate reason for the things that happen to you. However, this is only one aspect of the picture. The most important thing is your response to these situations.

Do you allow it to pound you down or make you feel numb to the point of submission? Do you let it cause you to be angry and bitter or overwhelm you with anxiety?

Or are you looking at it as a source of optimism? Each moment you triumph over a challenge you are proud of your personal strength over reality.

Do you feel hopeful from the fact that you're capable of conquering? Then, from this optimism you can find the motivation to continue living your life, aiming higher, and preparing to take on the bigger monsters and demons from your past to achieve higher and higher levels.

It's your choice. You can opt to be a victim -- like the majority of people at various levels, or you can take a different approach and choose to win.

Many people think of their desire through the lens of an external force

Another reason people fail to assert the power of their desires lies in the place they find the desire.

The majority of people think that the desire is similar to happiness. If things are good for them, people treat them with respect and things are in their favor and they are happy. When things get a bit rocky and problems arise the people are less content. What's the problem with this picture?

If you base your happiness or your capacity to be in a state of desire, based on the events going on around you, including situations and people you can't influence, then you'll continue to be in a struggle. You're waiting for everything else to become a reality.

The issue is that you can't control the variables. You're placing yourself in a position where you'll only grant yourself the permission to be happy or have a desire to experience better things when circumstances coincide to your advantage.

I'm telling youthat it's probably best to whip out a set of dice and continue throwing the dice. You're just dependent on the blind chance.

Truth about the desire

Desire doesn't come from external stimuli. It is instead the result of your choice. Whatever is good or bad or are becoming bleak, it shouldn't be a factor.

Desire is a method that is available for you to utilize if you want it. It's a heightened emotional and psychological experience that can trigger.

There is no need to wait around for that relationship to change. There is no need to address problems from your childhood or previous relationships in order to tap the potential of desire. You don't need to change jobs or find a more favourable boss to be able to feel the attraction in your life.

In reality, it's something that was always under your control. However, you didn't recognize the power of it. Instead, you've conceived it as an opportunity created by circumstances and people you are unable to influence.

It's yours. It is your birthright. capacity to want. It's part of human nature. All of us are born with this capability. Unfortunately, many of us try to squander it. Or, putting it in the hands of other people or believing that it's somehow unattractive, ugly and unappealing.

Let yourself go of this mental prison and realize that your desire is your service. It's not the one you serve or a kind prohibited fruit. It isn't a product that comes from somewhere outside. It is instead an instrument that you are able to easily access from wherever you are any time.

Chapter 2: The Importance Self-Love

Moments in time when you stop, gaze at yourself in the mirror and be able to appreciate your body.
An idea that increases your worth, your value. It is a decision to not be a sponge for the toxic energy of the boss you work for.
The option to purchase the sweet treat you've always wanted.
There are many examples of what self-love could appear like. That's just one person!

The concept of self-love is completely personal. It is possible to not connect with the idea of a spa day, but you can imagine a relaxing day in the river with cool water rushing over your head. The only simple and fast rule for self-love is that there aren't any strict and unchanging guidelines. It's about being yourself and acknowledging the things your body and your mind require.
Self-love is different for each person, but that doesn't mean that it isn't always simple. A lot

of people were raised in homes with toxic parents, led life situations that permitted abusive behavior or simply didn't know how to be themselves. Most of the time, these are aspects we learned from our parents as children. If you are feeling angry towards those who taught you, it could be beneficial to take the time to practice some practices that help release these feelings. If we hold on to the emotions of hate, anger or resentment, they can cause us to block our way from being the person we're supposed to be. It could be self-love to engage in practices that can help you let those emotions go. If you don't let go of the things that other people have done to us, it's an uphill road towards self-love.

Self-love is a path that is distinctive. In truth, it's an extremely difficult path for many people. The most important question to ask yourself is: What is self-love like and what does it mean to you?

Self-love may appear like any of the following:
* Prioritizing yourself
* Silenced self-shaming thoughts
* Be confident in yourself

* Believe in yourself
* Healthy boundaries and whole
* Engage in conversation with love and kindness to yourself

An effective way to start in the practice of self-love is by going back to the basics of our bodies and our minds. Some ideas for loving yourself can be found in the following list.

* Everyday stretching
* Spending time grooming yourself by painting your nails, braiding your hair or shaving your hair
* Being creative. Do you enjoy painting? Singing? Dancing? Do you?
* Strolls through the park
* sitting on a bench, taking in the beauty of the beauty of nature
* A solo trip
* We are having an evening of pasta and wine

The reasons for the focus on self-love is extensive. They can be extremely individualistic. There are a number of reasons the reasons to engage in self-love are being aware and being aware of yourself. If you don't have self-love and recognize your desires, it can be a difficult journey to becoming more generous. Self-love also allows the time to practice healthy habits such as exercising, resting and eating healthy. To be yourself is spending time with yourself. It is possible that you are an individual who is very extroverted. This is great and we appreciate the fact that. You may be dealing with a deep-seated anxiety and feel like you're not able to be yourself. It's okay too. It is possible to feel an increase in anxiety while you go through. However, whether we enjoy it or not, it's an essential practice to find a place to relax and be with yourself.

There are a few methods of becoming familiar with your self are listed below.

* Be still. It might take some time to sit still, but it's an excellent exercise. If we don't regularly practice times when you are seated and quiet in silence what will we do to distinguish ourselves from the people we're always around? Extroverts are also welcome here, but be aware that it's beneficial to be on your own. People who are introverts might struggle with sitting at a distance. Many

prefer to be on their own, but don't have time to talk about themselves. The difference lies in the effort you do. Being home on your own and constantly checking your smartphone or in front of the TV does not mean that you're not doing anything else.

Recognize who you are and not only who you'd like to be. This is an important one. A lot of us have the notion of who that we should be. Don't be a slave to that, it's not worth the time. It's possible that you have a great company job but have been tempted to give the whole thing up and settle out in the middle of the wilderness. Perhaps it's the complete opposite. Being still with yourself can help you determine what you are and what comes from your cultural influences or those that surround you. We all have pressures from family or friends who have pushed (or made) us to take a one that isn't our personal. Be aware that it could lead to burnout if you persist on the same way. Relax, hang around with yourself, and consider what are your needs and desires, and not the desires of others. If you are unsure of what to do to discover your personality, you can conduct the test of your personality. There are many types of tests that reveal the person we are and what we are like. It's not a shame to accept your zodiac sign, or way of working. It's a fantastic tool!

• Find out what you're skilled at and what you're not skilled at. It's okay to be free to know that you're not naturally gifted at basketball. That doesn't mean you shouldn't play with your friends however it gives you the ability to not put too high pressure on yourself while playing. This isn't an excuse to stop doing things that aren't natural to you, but it should provide you with the confidence to not put as much demands on yourself. Additionally, in this way knowing your strengths can inspire you to continue to study the things you enjoy. Perhaps you're very good with numbers and you love these things, but none of your friends are artists. There is no need to to be an artist if you don't like it. Accept what you're great at and let go of the things you think you ought to be skilled at. What's your greatest passion? It's all about discovering your strengths however there's a distinction. Perhaps you're not an expert at painting, but are passionate about painting. That's great! Hone your passions. Being aware of what you're interested in gives you an insight into your personality and also allows ideas to come into your self-love routine. Feedback is essential. It isn't easy for some to figure out the point at which they end and where other people close to them start. Find a trusted and trustworthy acquaintances to talk about the person they perceive and believe that you are. This can help to discover who you really are, and also to build confidence in yourself. A few questions you can ask your friends and acquaintances you trust include "What do you think the most important aspects of my strengths?" Always ask them what they think your weaknesses as. In order to be successful you must be honest and trusting of the person you're asking. You must ensure that they trust and respect you.

• Know your connections. The most important aspect of getting to know you is the people you surround yourself with. The same is true for relationships. If you don't understand yourself, then you'll never understand the people around you. If you don't take time to look into your personal being, how are you going to be able to appreciate the people that surround you? If you're currently in an intimate relationship, but haven't paid attention to yourself, you might find yourself in a situation that you do not want. If you're not sure who are, how do you know who you'd like to be around?

It's not easy to sit with yourself and your thoughts, looking over your thoughts and your childhood, worries and interests, but when the process is broken down,, all you're doing is having fun with yourself! You're probably thinking "Why do I need to spend time with me, since nobody else would want to be in my company?", then you are in a place where it is essential to be spending time with yourself. You are valuable and are able to contribute something for the rest of humanity. If you don't spend time with yourself, and acknowledging these things about yourself, you'll be unable to allow

people to see these qualities within you.
One great rule to remember is to complete tasks because you love your interests and not just because you feel you must get them completed. The pressure of obligations and expectations we carry from our daily activities can be exhausting and, often, we lose sight of the person we really are and what we really need. Self-love can bring us back to the things that matter and protects our minds and bodies from exhaustion.

The value of self-love is a proven asset in the process of implementing The Law of Attraction. Some may call the process"the "Law of Love". It can be a long and difficult journey discovering how to love yourself.

The Mind

Let's begin by focusing on the importance of the mind with regard to self-love. Our brain can be a huge reservoir, however it's not designed to store everything in. The emotions are the gateway to the heart, and understanding the way you're experiencing is crucial so that your brain can be able to release tension and expectations. If your mind is holding the negative emotions within it, it will only cause lasting negative vibrations that attract more negative energy. Release negative emotions to the world will release those harmful negative emotions that are buried within.

A simple way to begin an process of letting go of negative feelings is to start by speaking it out. Have a person join you as you work through your emotions. Perhaps you're processing your emotions internally and prefer to talk to an object of paper regarding your emotions. Incorporating professional assistance like a counselor is an effective method to assist your mind let go of negative thoughts. All of these methods can help your mind get rid of weight off of it and put it to rest. Your mind can do plenty and, with that said, it doesn't require additional burdens that weigh it down. Relax and let your mind breathe in a fresh air by letting go of negative thoughts. In Chapter 4, we'll discuss practicing meditation in a way and the ways the process can greatly aid in relaxing your mind.

A few people might require more extensive ways to help your mind discover self-love. Therapy sessions are available one could consider if they are in need.

Eye Movement Desensitization Reprocessing (EMDR) or EMDR is a kind of therapy that directly connects with the brain. It was invented in the latter half of the 20th century, and can help let go of emotional tensions that usually originate from traumatic events that have occurred that have occurred in their lives. Simply put, it can be carried out in a variety of sessions. The patient will be seated with an therapist, and they will recount the events that traumatized the patient through either talking or through the mind. The patient will use various types of stimulants to use during this process like vibrators in their hands, or other methods like rub a arm or leg constantly. After a brief time the therapist will direct the patient's brain to focus on something totally not related. The cycle of reliving the trauma as well as physical stimulation helps the brain to let go of stress.

This kind of counselor can be beneficial to those who have an unfavorable view of self or has experienced an emotional trauma or has other problems in their lives that prevent your ability to live a life of freedom. More details on EMDR is available online at the EMDR Institute (see EMDR Institute for more information).

Naturally, there are those who require assistance with their mental capabilities by taking medication. Depression, Anxiety, Obsessive Compulsive Disorder (OCD), Attention-Deficit/Hyperactivity Disorder (ADHD), and many other life-prohibiting stressors can cause someone to not be able to give self-love to their minds.

The use of EMDR and medications could be the route you'll need to follow to discover self-love and take taking care of your mind. There is also the possibility of having someone who's willing to assist you in walking through difficult thoughts and convictions you've got. Both are beautiful ways to let your mind know that you cherish and value it.

If you're one of those who prefers to settle in

the quiet of a cafe and put your thoughts on paper and write it down, then I completely understand. There are tons in journals, prompts and tips on ways to practice self-love and self-care by writing it out.

Let's look at some prompts for your journal to help you write about what's on your mind!

Journal Prompts:

1. What are my feelings regarding myself when I am sitting here?
2. What would the day look like if I truly self-loved and respected?
3. What do I think self-love is like? What is it like to feel?
4. Are there any worries I'm having to deal with for the day? Which ones are these? What is the reason I am feeling anxious?
5. What can I do to advocate for and inspire self-love in my mind during my day this moment?
6. What are the things I should consider to refuse?
7. Who inspires me? What makes me feel inspired?
8. What are five things I am grateful for

today?

9. Can I get help from other people easily?

10. What can I do to block the desire to love myself?

11. How can I compare myself with others, and how do I let go of the ones?

12. What do I hold opinions about myself?

13. What's the greatest thing I've made to myself?

14. Do I have something I would like people would praise about me? Can I speak about self-love in those areas?

15. What aspects of me do I wish to modify? Could I change them in a manner that encourages positive feelings and appreciation towards these specific things?

16. What hurdles have I had to overcome?

Understanding how you process and release your emotions is an excellent method to begin the process of self-love. Numerous psychologists believe that bottled emotions can lead to self-inflicted negative thoughts. Therefore, figuring out early how to face the emotions you feel will be beneficial in the end. Keep in mind that you're doing an excellent job and that the fact that are here, taking the time to get to know your own self along with your own Law of Attraction is something to be proud of in yourself.

The Heart

The next step in self-love is to acknowledge the heart. As you process and shed emotions from your brain Be aware of the way you present the emotions you feel has the greatest impact on the self-love you show. If you are in a counseling facility there could be a myriad of emotions that arise within your heart. This is normal and means that you're working hard to be the best person you can be from now on.

A lot of us are told that negativity is negative emotions. This isn't always the case. Anger is a feeling that informs our heart and mind about what's happening beneath the surface. It is usually a sign that we feel that there is a lack of respect for the person or thing. In order to push these feelings under the surface, and not acknowledge them implies that we will remain in the state of feeling the same way. They may surface in various forms which are insensitive to the individual or the situation. If you're in a disagreement against your manager at work due to the fact that they have reneged regarding a promise they made to you and you're upset, resolve the issue. If you don't, the anger may resurface through the form of passive aggressive behavior, leading to more workplace issues.

If you are feeling that your emotions and heart are sending you worries or fears take note of the thoughts. It might be nothing but it could be the brain taking over the truth of what the situation is telling you. However, it could also be something worth paying attentively to. You are a good judge of yourself, and if you feel your intuition is very accurate, then listen to them. Let's say that you can go on two different routes returning home at night. You could take a walk through a park to enjoy peace and quiet, or stroll down to the main road. Perhaps you usually follow the paths through the park, but this particular evening, you're feeling some anxiety over that choice. Follow your gut and don't dismiss them as irrelevant. Be aware of the voice of your heart to you.

Another method of checking in with your heart to examine your intentions. If you are sitting in a conversation with a acquaintance, take a look at your heart. Are you able speak at a calm level to them in the event that they have questions which do not be helpful for the situation you are? You could be entering the conversation or in a situation that you're aware won't help you over the long term. The motives you are expressing could be fueled by anger or anger or. Saying something in a cruel or unkind manner won't remove the negative emotions from your body and will only keep them in your mind. Similar to that, entering into a situation that you are aware of isn't good for your body or you is not going to benefit you over the long haul. Be aware of the motives within your mind and make decisions based on them.

To cultivate self-love by using your practice of the Law of Attraction, focus on the words that your heart is telling you. Release the positive magnetic energy you're working towards the person that you are talking to. The Universe will be grateful for what you're putting out to the world, and you'll see an increase in self-love. You could even be aiding the person you're communicating with on the path to your Law of Attraction.

Beware of accepting negativity into your heart from other people as well. If you meet your trusted friend only to have them break your trust with their negativity or lack of empathy be aware of the way this affects your heart, and then take positive actions. Remember, when someone speaks negatively or negative towards you, they are likely to have harsher opinions toward themselves. What other people say about or about you doesn't necessarily reflect your personality. Make sure you are confident in who consider yourself to be and you'll be less likely to be influenced by what others believe or say. Everyone is magnetic, regardless of whether they believe it or not. Your step is to be aware of what they're releasing to the world and then react in accordance with where you are on your own journey.

Chapter 3: Analyzing your current situation and the gap between your current circumstances and your goal

Understanding your current position relative to your vision and goal is crucial.

The process of evaluating and accepting the current situation in this specific area that you live in directly affects the level of achievement.

Let's say that you want to make more money in your life. It is important to understand the limits you are currently facing. What is your earnings and what amount would you like to earn within a certain time frame?

The most important thing to consider is how you came to be to where you are and the severity of your present situation is of no significance to The Law of Attraction. The sensation you experience when you are from calculating your debt and income is often overwhelming. The feeling can be a source of anxiety and getting caught up in how dire the situation and judging yourself, then reveling in guilt and anger over the situation, and then blaming yourself for financial mistakes hinders the momentum, energy and creativeness to organize, manifest and progress. Be open to accepting your reality and recognizing the flaws in a non-judgmental manner and the joy of achieving the desired results doing the right thing will place your mind in a place that you are able to think positive thoughts. and manifest the goals you'd like to achieve and achieve over a specific amount of time.

The universe is the source of energy. Its energy flows through you, so everything you think or feel is connected to the energy source.

By creating the positive feeling of neutrality about what was happening in the past you are telling your energy source that you're ready for something different from what was happening in the past.

Accepting the current circumstance it is easier to accept that mistakes don't define you and that you can learn from them. Therefore, you're worthy of love, no matter the circumstance. It won't become real until you accept that truth.

The universe doesn't need to show any thing to anyone. It's your thoughts, behavior and emotions that create and transforms in the direction of energy in order to fulfill your goals.

It is the first thing to concentrate so that you are able to precisely target this massive and pure energy.

The second step is to be able to accept and comprehend the reality of the present and current events without anger, resentment or guilt.

The attitude of gratitude for the present is

exactly what you should to be thankful for. This is the real meaning of love, and the fact that you are aware of the events you experienced in the past are your guide to achieving the things you want.

Chapter 4: The Role of Vibration as well as belief systems in the Law of Attraction

If you want to learn a bit more about bioenergy, I'd recommend you check this free gift.

Because everything is made of energy, and energy is constantly moving and interacting, you'll experience energy fields that influence one another. This is how it is that attraction law functions. In the event that your energetic state operating at the same level that chocolate does, you will feel attracted to chocolate, and it will also be drawn to you. It may sound strange, but it's actually true. Perhaps you've thought about a friend that you haven't been in contact with for many years. What is it that you are thinking about this person so frequently these days? The reason is that both of you have the same frequency of energy. In no time when both of you remain attuned to the energy of each other then you'll get an email from the person you are calling. Imagine what number of times that this scenario has occurred? Isn't that scary? You might happen to encounter him in the streets or make the effort to make a gesture to him.

Here's a straightforward example of similar energies drawing one another, which happens to many people.

There is a song you love in the air. You sing along to the music while it plays and it puts you in a great mood. When you're content instead of sadness, filled with happiness and joy instead of anger or frustration Your nervous system notices. It starts to affect your energy to make you are at the same frequency as the music you enjoy. The joy you feel is akin to and happiness.

Before you even realize it, you're listening to the song all over the place. It's a song that you are drawn to and it's drawing to you. What happens next is that you contemplate this song at an upcoming time and then it comes up on the radio. It's likely that it has happened several times as well!

As we said earlier that this could be to your advantage. If your energy is vibrating with a frequency which is similar to alcohol or drugs, you can guess what you'll desire, even if you're not physically dependent. You might be wondering what causes you drawn to the wrong type of relationship. You are likely to be in unhealthy relationships that are not fulfilling and could even be hazardous.

It is true that you're attracted to that unsuitable partner, and you will always attract that type of ... till you alter the frequency in your life. This is right, you could alter how your energy reverberates to ensure that you attract things you desire.

For a recap the law of attraction facts:

* Everything is energy.
* Energy oscillates at certain frequency.
* Frequency patterns that are similar attract to one another because they align.

You can alter the frequency of your energy to attract the things you want.

We will then discuss the reasons you could be attracting negative experiences towards yourself. Although we might try and would like to attract positive energy, we could draw negative energy too. Learn how to stop believing in beliefs that lead to negative outcomes.

How Can Limiting Beliefs Draw the opposite of what you Would Like

Limiting your thoughts will eventually keep you from achieving your goals. They prevent you from creating the that you've always wanted to be. When you consider it, it doesn't make much sense on the surface. Why is it that people continue to develop belief systems that can lead to negative outcomes? Most people have beliefs that prevent them from being all they could be, however they also dream of fulfillment, success, and prosperity.

What is the reason these negative thinking patterns appear to overpower more positive beliefs? What is the reason that negativity is so powerful in our minds?

One theory is that if the brain isn't engaged or engaged, it will return to negative thinking patterns This is a normal human default mode. To give an extreme case of this, the following scenario can be used: Take two people. One is on a boat drinking champagne while taking pleasure in the sun's rays. Another one is working as a cleaner, and cleaning the toilet. Who is the more happy? Everyone will recommend the one who is lying on the boat enjoying a drink while relaxing. But, if we look back to the topic we previously discussed and find that a mind unoccupied tends to revert back to negative thoughts, then we are in the wrong.

The person who is cleaning the toilets will be more content at the moment as their mind is only focused on the task at hand and not thinking about the possible catastrophes could befall them. However someone sitting on the boat without anything to think about will eventually begin thinking about what might be wrong and disrupt their relaxing.

One of the main reasons that has been proved by scientific research is that people are inherited negative behaviors and mental models from earlier generations. However, the reverse could be valid. Your parents may have developed values or ideas that led to amazing and positive reality which you also have inherited.

This is typically the case for people who cannot seem to accomplish something wrong. This could be frustrating, since you're trying so hard to build a perfect life but you aren't able to achieve it, while these people seem to live their lives without conscious thought. What is the cause and what's the solution to this apprehension?

Genetics is the answer, and is proven by with the help of mice and cherry blossoms.

Brian Dias and his team of scientists at Emory University School of Medicine in Atlanta believed that the experiences of the past affected the physical constitution of the next generation. One example pertains to people who were a part of the Dutch food shortage of 1944.

Many of the people who survived the horrific famine went on become parents. Their children were significantly smaller birth weights, and had more health issues than was normal. The children of that generation also suffered from similar health problems. It could be that those who survived the famine associated their surroundings with the negative experience of their lives and then passed this conviction onto the next generation?

Dias believed so. He as well as the Dr. Kerry Ressler had mice detect the scent of cherry blossoms. When they were smelling the scent mice were subjected to mild but evident electric shocks. Additionally, there were mice who were either exposed to other scent, or to no scent at all.

The mice from the cherry blossoms mated. The next mouse generation was exposed fragrance of the cherry blossoms for the very first time. While they didn't know about the cherry blossoms, or the scent they released The mice of the earliest days were extremely sensitive to the scent. They were able to detect it in very tiny quantities and would stay clear of it as much as they could. Mice that were born into the control group who didn't undergo the cherry blossom conditioning , responded in a normal way to the smell. This is how evolution operates.

The most amazing part is the fact that the second-generation mice born to first-generation offspring of the blossom mice also carried the genetic disposition of not liking the scent of cherry blossoms. This study appeared in 2013, in the Nature Neuroscience journal.

The genetic modifications that alter composition before birth are referred to as epigenetic processes. This means that exposure or environment can trigger the binding of specific chemical compounds to the genes. This acts as an alarm system that gets transferred onto the genes of future generations.

Research was conducted to determine whether the mice relayed the negative experience they had to their children, but it was not the scenario. The mice that were trained to fear the cherry blossoms had more chemical receptors that are sensitive to the odor of the cherry blossoms. This confirmed that the condition is transmitted through genetics and rather than through communicating or any different method of instruction.

This indicates that self-limiting beliefs and anxieties can be naturally acquired. They can be inherited via your ancestral tree. The good news is that beliefs restricting your progress can be altered. It is possible to believe of abundance and happiness and transfer this belief onto your children, while creating the ideal reality you seek. As much as we are able to pass on anxiety and fears as well, we can also transmit positive emotions, too.

How to change self-limiting beliefs by using LOA

If you're a victim of a belief system that is creating an unfavorable reality on your behalf, that could be a powerful one and difficult to get rid of. What you've learned is that it could be a belief system that has been handed down over generations. The genetic makeup of your body believes this is how the world functions. It is your natural reaction to specific environments events, experiences or situations due to the way in which you were wired. This could be harmful to your wellbeing and health and eventually your future.

Sometimes, we form false beliefs as a result of being exposed to a certain type of trauma as a young child. Even when you are an adult you can respond by expressing negative, neutral or positive emotions to anything that occurs to you. You've been programmed to react in negative ways , and do it in your subconscious.

If you emit negative vibes due to the experience you've had the universe starts to expose you to another kind of experience. This is why you appear to be in a state of trance at times. However hard you try, you'll never break free from a vicious negative cycle. A self-fulfilling prophecy if you like.

Many people go through their lives not knowing what they can do to change their life. After many years of living like this they believe that it's their fate in life and there's no way to change it.

There is no way to tell the truth however. You

can alter the frequency in which your energy vibrates. It is a simple and natural change in the things you begin attracting and noticing. It is all you need to do is exert your willpower and direct your attention and energy to create a positive physical reality. It starts by focusing on the correct thinking.

Chapter 5: What you can do to apply the Law of Attraction to find love

Love is among the most complicated emotions for an individual and, consequently, it is one of the hardest emotions for normal people to display and receive without becoming totally insane. It is the Law of Attraction allows us to choose the love deserves to be ours and then respond with a positive attitude, creating an enjoyable relationship for us and our partner. We have already learned about what is the Law of Attraction is, how to incorporate it into our lives and guide the universe to the best vibrations we emit through our unconscious and conscious.

The first step to finding the perfect partner in your life is to know what you are looking for and deserve. If you don't know what you're looking for then you'll never find the perfect person to live your life with. When you know what you are looking for in terms of relationships, you will know the energy that you would like to broadcast into the universe . This is the initial step in The Law of Attraction.

Once you've set your thoughts about what you want to find it's time to move onto the next step , which is to focus your thoughts on the ideal vibrations you would like to broadcast out to the universe. This can be accomplished by one or more of the three techniques we talked about earlier: meditation or affirmations, as well as the practice of hypnosis. Being a part of in the Law of Attraction when it is about finding the right partner also involves making lifestyle changes. You have to live your life in a way that you're willing to allow the possibility of an integral part of your life. One way to accomplish this include using only the half of your closet and sleeping on one side of your bed, or even buying an auto for your family. With these little changes, it will signal to the universe and the person you are considering to marry that you're prepared to have a serious relationship at the end of your life. When you have made these changes, make sure you change your personal self too. Make sure you take your care of yourself so that you're the ideal candidate for someone who is looking for their future partner. Make sure you take good care of your physical appearance by going to a gym as well as dressing appropriately and responsibly or picking a pastime which you can enjoy with your prospective partner. Take a look at your life from a different angle. Do you have the qualifications and professional experience that is attractive to the kind of partner you're seeking? Are you living in a glam bachelor pad or are you with the start of a new family? If you're looking to prepare yourself for the family life and a more mature lifestyle, ensure that you're already living it.

You must be doing daily meditation on the partner you would like to have to have in your life, and finding confidence that you are the perfect partner. Think about your character and willingness to share the love you deserve. Your attitude toward love is vital to the energy you transmit to the universe. If you don't believe that you deserve love , or think you are entitled to the wrong type of love, then you are not in the right place. Law of Attraction will not be in your favor.

Every day , you can use affirmations toward love. Believe in yourself that you're worthy of trusting and unwavering love to come to your world. Say to yourself that you're willing to welcome that love into your life in a completely unrestricted way. Make sure to speak out positive viewpoints regarding the love you've been looking for all your life, and the universe will return it to you in response to the vibrations you emit.

Finally, align your thoughts to your goals every day. It is important to let your inner self accept the changes in your life so that the vibrations you transmit to the universe are ones you wish to see coming back to you. The use of hypnosis is an extremely well-known method for getting this done. Hypnosis enters the subconscious and alters the root of our thinking pattern, changing the frequencies we transmit out to the world.

The love you've always wanted is in your grasp. You're able to empower you to be able to attain everything you could ever imagine was possible. Your mind is more powerful than you could ever imagine and more powerful than you've been taught to believe. With your mind's Law of Attraction you can bring about any change you'd like to possible within your life. With a focus and belief in yourself, you can alter your profession, your mindset and your outlook on life. You can discover true love by taking control of your emotions and thoughts. What is known as the Law of Attraction is your path to the life that you believed was only possible in your imagination. You're as gorgeous as handsome, attractive, confident, and prosperous as you believe is feasible. You possess the most incredible potential within you. This ability can get you the opportunity you've been wanting for a long time and the house you have images of on your wall, the relationship of your dreams.

This is the perfect moment to control the things you've always dreamed of the future, and everything you've learned is within your reach. You are the creator of your destiny, however it's your responsibility to take the pen and begin writing. You can dream bigger than you imagined could be possible. Don't give up on anything less than the best Do not be afraid to take a stand in your goals. Your Law of Attraction is now your power and is your most effective weapon.

Chapter 6: LoA and Personal Growth

LoA and its objectives

If you're like many people, you make goals every day but never achieve these goals. For instance, many people will make an annual resolution for the year but fail to keep it up. You could be in the same boat.

If you're interested in making a change, then Find a way to ensure you meet your goals. The Law of Attraction can change your life.

What is the reason? because the LoA is a matter of goals and accomplishments. It is a known truth that the distinction between those who are successful and those who fail is usually a tiny margin. People who succeed are determined to stick with their aim for a while and those who did not quit.

In this regard, let's look at two ways you can use the LoA to meet your own personal goals in life.

Example # 1: Weight loss

Perhaps you've been trying shed 20 pounds over the several years, but aren't able to. Never had success. You tried this several times but haven't followed through. The application of the LoA can help you reach this goal without much effort, effort, and battle.

It is possible to begin by fixing your attention on the objective of weight reduction. Choose a goal which must be accomplished. Find reasons that support this decision and continually remind yourself of these motivations.

After you've genuinely decided that the mission is worthy of the effort, you will be able to achieve it.
that it brings that it brings, you can move on to the visual you will experience, shift to the visualization phase. Imagine the results you'll gain the weight. Imagine yourself working out

in the gym, and making difficult choices in your diet that will require sacrifice.

Furthermore, think about how these changes will enhance your life. Visualize yourself in the near future when you have lost weight. Do you feel more healthy? Feel less self-conscious? Are you feeling more confident and attractive?

These are all crucial things to consider and understand. There is no better method to accomplish this than by using the LoA. Remember: if you would like to draw a more slim version of yourself in your daily life You will need to focus your thoughts on this image.

Then, you must be open to the attainment of the objective. When you encounter those baffling
instances when you suddenly have to ask about whether it is really you desire to become 20 pounds smaller, you can declare that this is your goal from the beginning.

You're confident that you've made the right choice Do not allow yourself to be in conflict, and let the rug be pulled away from you.

2. Personal development

Sometimes, we are bored of the status quo and begin to think about
What our lives would be like if we invested the time to build an ability or learn how to do a trade. For instance, you could consider what life would have been as if you kept playing the saxophone or had he learned more about the art of.

These are all valid desires and each has the potential of personal development and increased happiness in your life. However, if If we are ever hoping to enjoy the pleasure when playing an instrument with proficiency or try a new art with a professional, we'll have to invest time and effort in order to enhance our abilities.

Fortunately the LoA clearly explains how to

do this. Start by deciding on what we want to accomplish and when we have made that decision then we can set our aim. For instance, you decide you'd like to learn how to play the Saxophone.

However, if you don't think this is something you'd like to accomplish and you don't want to set it as the goal. Make it an aim if it's something you want to achieve in your life and it's something you believe can improve your life by a tangible way.

Once you have your goal set and the goal in mind, think about how you can accomplish it. Are you going to perform it three times a week? Are you going to do it in the morning, or do it at night? Do you plan to invite your family members to be part of the practice? Do you plan to meet other musicians to join them on the instrument?

Then, you must be willing to achieve the objective. Imagine that it is an entire year away and you are an expert musician on the saxophone. What are your thoughts about this idea? Do you feel uncomfortable about it? Are you feeling dissatisfied as if you were only looking forward to the hunt and not in the end result?

You must overcome these anxieties. The last stage of the LoA is to feel comfortable with your accomplishment of your goals. This is exactly what you must do in order to be successful.

Learning and LoA

The last thing we'll take into consideration one more is LoA as well as the learning. This is vital since learning disabilities are usually the reason why people aren't successful. They are not prepared to learn and evolve when they grow or do not want to master something that allows them to develop and make better decisions.

In the end following to the LoA will be the same like always. Make a decision about what you'll need to know or how you'll need to alter the way you learn (ie perhaps you'd like to keep learning continuously instead of focusing on one thing at a time in the way you do today).

When the goal is established and the goal is set, the process will be no different than any of the scenarios we've discussed up to now. Just visualize the outcome and then let yourself be open to the realization of the learning and the advantages it can provide.

Summary of Chapter

In this brief chapter, we've looked at the ways in which it is possible that the Law of Attraction can be applied to your personal development. Naturally the answer is the same as before. Start by defining your personal growth goals. After that follow the three steps to success.

Chapter 7: Making sense of affirmations

Do you want to learn the 7 magic systems for better life for free.

Affirmations are words that express pure intention. They can be used in a variety of ways, but, in the context of that law of attraction they're our appeal for the world to listen. They increase our desire and provide instructions to attract the things we desire to attract into our lives. We've talked about the advantages of optimism and it is possible to imagine affirmations as the next step in. Affirmations allow you to connect to the outer reaches that the law of attraction has. when you use them regularly you can begin to take control of your destiny in ways you never thought feasible. Affirmations are used to access the energy that forms the core of all things.

How do you make this work?

There are two aspects to consider when looking at our the thoughts. Law of Attraction offers both a religious explanation as well as an actual scientific explanation.

Spiritual

Since we all are composed of energy and that energy is able to operate at various frequency, the assumption exists that, we're, in fact, altering the frequency of our lives by altering our thinking patterns. Through positive affirmations and patterns of thought allow us to draw in or align our lives with God or any other religious beliefs. When we concentrate on a happy and hopeful future, we'll be able to bring more happiness to our lives. Therefore, what we draw depends on our thoughts or on the subject of our concentration, but the main thing is to believe that it is already ours or is in the process of becoming.

Science

The scientific explanation is more scientific, but it is in many aspects it is similar. One who is intent on transforming their life and truly believes it is possible, tends to take on greater risk and consequently taking more chances. This typically results in them noticing opportunities and becoming ready to leap. Positive attitude builds and they continue to find new opportunities.

It operates in the same manner in reverse. If someone doesn't believe that things will be good then they are more likely to avoid taking risks or avoiding opportunities altogether.

We all know people who drastically changed their lives. They have improved their finances as well as their homes, their relationships or careers. they might have achieved this through a shift in thinking and made a decision or, perhaps they were able to tap on the laws of attraction.

Is affirmation a verb?

Your affirmations are the thoughts you think about which express your intention. If you write affirmations that have meaning in your life, it allows you to connect to the energy that is part of all things. If you repeat these phrases or listen to them, they hold the ability to shape your personal reality. Positive affirmations transform optimism into superdrive.

A typical person is able to have about 300 to 300 thoughts per minute that go through their brains and research has revealed that as high as to 80% of those thoughts could be negative. This is awe-inspiring. Most thoughts , or the greatest percent of them are unconscious thoughts that are beyond the conscious mind. Affirmations are affirmations that help you become aware of these thoughts and help you gain the ability to control them.

You are exactly what you imagine.

If we accept the findings of that research, then all the negative thoughts that whirl around our minds can have a negative impact on what we want to draw. When we affirm ourselves and affirmations, we can take a deliberate approach to changing. This puts us in control , and also more conscious about our thinking. We gain awareness of thoughts that are hidden. It's similar to having an oar that you could paddle the water however, in the absence of it, your voyage could not be as effective or feasible.

What we're trying to achieve is to free ourselves from the routine of our lives that we live in and move about without guidance. It is time to get out of the hole which becomes a daily routine, in order to recognize the journey we have to undertake. Thoughts have the power to be incredibly powerful. We need to be in control of the things we truly believe in otherwise negative thoughts that get as a result of doubts could hinder us from achieving our goals. However, we shouldn't allow negative thoughts to rule our lives. The word "affirmation" means to indicate intent. It refers to stating an event in a positive manner.

Affirmations should be written down to be repeated positive manner. They must have been written in a manner that suggests they are valid. This is crucial because if you're asking for something, then you already declare that you do not have the item. Like attracts like If you recall our earlier example.

Remember that affirmations bring you into the forefront of your thoughts but it also allows you to have more control over them. This can lead to your own awakening. Your affirmations should reflect your intention that the truth is already there.

There's a huge differences between the phrase:

"I would like to feel happy', rather than"I am happy.'

The way to think about affirmations is to consider them as sentences created to connect with the subconscious and conscious mind. If we repeat affirmations we conjure up images that could be motivating and inspiring. Continuously repeating these words of intention embeds the message into our subconscious mind, which then reflects on our actions and changes the energy that surrounds us.

When is the best time to use affirmations?

If you can, it's recommended to set aside the time every throughout the day to say your affirmations over and over again. Personalizing your affirmations by writing them out yourself is the best way to go since you are writing from your inside of your heart, and with conviction. Repetition of affirmations and reading them with intention is crucial. Start in the morning and the last in the evening, but you are able to use affirmations at any point. The more often you use them, the more powerful the impact.

Although it's best to speak them loudly but you can also use them in a quiet manner, but be sure to think about the tone and the intention while doing so.

Create affirmations into as a positive habit. They are effective.

Be sure to believe in what you're doing, as doubts only hinder your progress which is why so many fail when it comes to using the law of attraction.

There's no standard regarding how often you should say affirmations. However, the general guideline is that if you believe in them and continue to practice the affirmations, you'll be able to reinforce this inner message. Just a few minutes in the middle of your day can be extremely beneficial for you. You must affirm it with passion, love and genuine enthusiasm because this can greatly accelerate your progress.

It is a process that takes time to master, and you must commit to this tested method since there's no reason to believe that it shouldn't perform for you, too.

Chapter 8: DETERMINING and UTILIZING A GROWTH MINDSET

The mindset is the self-perception we generally believe about ourselves. It is the place you can find people who think they are smart and others who believe they're not. It is not necessary to discern your thinking but it has an impact on your performance. The two most commonly used types of minds are fixed and growth , and those with a fixed mentality believes that their core skills like intelligence or talent are inherently fixed. However, when you have a growth mindset, you are aware that there is always an opportunity to improve. A growth-oriented person will are also convinced that success requires effort and talent.

The greatest benefit of developing a growth mentality is that you will be better prepared to face any new challenge that comes your way because you are aware that talent and skills can be created through dedication and hard work. Any goal shouldn't sound more daunting than you can achieve since if you think about it , then you'll be able to accomplish it. There are many advantages associated with the mindset of growth and the most significant is that it fosters the desire to learn and the level of perseverance required for success.

A growth mindset is associated with enthusiasm and improved productivity. If you have a connection with the most successful people you know, I I am sure you know what I'm talking about. In our daily lives we face every kind of challenge and have to face more difficult situations than we did before. It doesn't mean that where you've gotten to, it's out of your reach This means you need to push your limits in your thinking process and the effort you put into and so on. Nothing is ever impossible in the world of life. They simply become more difficult and provides a reason to constantly think outside the box.

If you live living with a rigid mentality there is a chance of not getting much done since to you, one is either great or bad at certain things. With a mindset of growth, it's much easier for anyone to realize that they are proficient in anything so it is a matter of putting into it more effort. As of now, I think that you are aware of the power of your mind and how it has the power to influence your daily life. Your beliefs could either stop the process from taking place or enable the development of new abilities.

Whatever you'd like to accomplish in any area of your life, you must begin with a growing mindset. Even as you might have a strategy in place, you don't know how the ideas come out. In order to achieve the success you'll have to adapt as well as learn new skills and most importantly alter the way you think. Anyone can become more intelligent through repetition and dedication.

If you're unable to manage a particular task does not mean you're a fool this is just a sign that you could improve your performance over what you could have done at the beginning. It's also an opportunity to increase your knowledge by pushing yourself harder and getting the assistance you require. Be willing to push you every day and in the end, it all , you'll be a better and smarter person.

Methods of Developing A GROWTH MINDSET
Sometimes it is difficult to maintain the growing mindset, that is understandable based on the stories we've experienced in life. However, the positive side is that it's likely to cultivate the mindset of growth and change everything in your life. All you have be able to follow these steps in order:
* Accept Failure: This is the time you have to alter how you deal with failure and the way you perceive it. Making it a more positive way of thinking allows you to create an optimistic mindset. When you fall short at something you'll want to not stop, but rather to push harder in order to improve your outcomes.
It is important to challenge yourself. It is recommended to avoid handling those easy tasks or projects that you know you'll never do well in. In times of need, it's better to think outside of the box and come up with new

opportunities. As a result, you will need to do more for your part and you'll have to be able to grow to be noticed.

Learn more This is yet another method by which you can achieve the mindset of growth. All you have to do is learn new things from time intervals. It could mean increasing your knowledge or abilities, and will enable you to take on more difficult tasks in life and allow you to achieve great results.

* Stop Trying to Get Approval You have a life to live, and by being in control of everything is not more important than your own. It is important to realize that the moment you start to focus on approval, you'll end up losing your ability to develop.

• Value Process Over End-Result The main thing is the journey that is important and if you are able to appreciate the effort you've put in, the effort into, it will become easier to recognize your capabilities and desire to develop your abilities.

Be positive about criticism No one knows the amount of work you put into it or how much effort you invest in something. Whatever you're doing, believe in yourself and, if you encounter criticism, way, try to look at them as constructive.

How can we harness our imagination to create our future?
If we've attracted or the world around us with our own thoughts, it means that the material creation of objects has been a spiritually inspired creation and that your future is created in your own mind.

What you believe, think and think about is often the base of the experiences you'll encounter in your life. Thoughts that germinate like seeds in the soil of your subconscious will form your future .

The most interesting part is that the thought itself is nothing more than the volts of current. Although the majority of us pay no thought to your thoughts, this little bit has a huge impact on our feelings, actions and the future. Although we may not be able to grasp them using our hands Our thoughts are the same as objects we see using our eyes. If we pay attention and pay attention, we will see our reality is real and the reality we do not doubt , is solely in our minds.

Think about the relationship you have with your partner , with your peers, your parents or children. What exactly does an intimate relationship look like? How authentic is it?

Are they in your life right now? If not does that mean your relationship with this person is not in place at the moment? No, of course it doesn't. The relationship continues regardless of their absence, doesn't it?

The relationship that you have this month exists only in your head. However, that doesn't mean it's not less than real. So, what's that relationship you have with the person? What thoughts do you have for her.

Beyond that the fact that everything that transpired until that point in your life is only within your head. Your thoughts, memories thoughts, beliefs, weaknesses, and anxieties are only in your mind. However, that doesn't make them less real.

I am reminded of a student that nearly collapsed during an exam in the University. He was like chalk in color and could not walk on his own and was forced to cancel the test. He was so scared of the test that it was a challenge for him to prove whether he had been able to comprehend the material or not. The tragedy was not based on his own thought patterns. He had focused so heavily on his fear and the possibility of failure that his thoughts took on a life of their own and manifested in his physical health. The negative power of his thought was enough to trigger physical changes to the body, which almost led to him falling. This is a perfect illustration of how we can hinder our progress by focusing our attention on events or ideas that cause self-destructive and harmful images.

When you fail or succeed there is a similar thing that happens either way: the one who believes and hopes that success will come to him and the person who believes and believes that he'll be unsuccessful are correct, since the ability to create either one or the other is within his head, in his mind. If you are someone who is unable to accomplish anything and constantly think about how they can't do it are constantly thinking about their weaknesses and never achieve their goals.

There are two key ideas about how our the future is shaped by our thoughts:
The first reason is that you will only be a part of your thinking. It's impossible to act with an idea that's not in your mind. I often see people who cannot provide a reason for why they were unsuccessful.

If I ask them what they'd like to accomplish and they aren't sure. What can you do to achieve goals you don't have? If you're looking to make something happen in your life, it is necessary to put it in your mind and imagine it. Keep in mind that each act is preceded by a thought.

The third realisation is that anything you think about will have an the center stage in your daily life and be manifested. What you think about is a reality. If you are focused on your weak points, they will become increasingly important to your daily life. If you constantly think about your flaws and weaknesses, you'll never let go of the belief that you're not good enough. The more incompetent you think you are, the more inadequate you'll be perceived and treated by your surroundings. Your surroundings will only confirm what you've already believed: You are a weak person. Are you aware of the dangers this vicious circle can be?
According to Albert Einstein already said: "The only true enemies of an individual are his negativity."

The same is true for our relationships. If you are constantly thinking about what your spouse is lacking, you will be able to be able to see the flaws more clearly and clearly each day. Do you want to see your kids doing things better and more effectively? Begin by giving them a surprise rewards if they have achieved something you're proud of. If you are focused on every single thing you don't do and you'll notice an improvement each day.

Right now you have the opportunity to create a brand new future that is full of prosperity, success and joy. All you need to do is alter the kind of thoughts that you've fed into your mind. Imagine the goals you'd like to realize. Consider the qualities and skills you wish to build. Consider the traits you would like to observe in yourself and others. You will be able to see how these ideas appear in your daily life.

The first step in using this law is to first understand is to start by establishing: A life, a conscious Thinking Consciously means to be present in the here and now and become conscious of how one is living. How you feel, think or express, and then implement. It is also about being able to be in the present moment. But, we are accustomed to living our lives elsewhere as opposed to present moment.

The past is a living thing

We often live in the past, and we think what would have been better had we taken this or that action. We dwell on regrets about the past, and better times, and then resent ourselves for the allegedly wrong choices we've made. We squander our time by reliving painful memories of things which are decades away but we don't let ourselves sleep soundly in the night. The past can trigger sadness, guilt and self-loathing.

"Why did I not ask her? This would have been THE chance to meet my soulmate. I was just cowardly and shrewd."

"That wasn't a great idea to discuss it publicly before my boss. I'll never be a bit embarrassed about my promotion."

"The slice of cake tasted delicious. But, I shouldn't have had dessert in the first place.

Typical. I didn't stick to my eating habits during three consecutive days. The summer is near and I'm not going to be rid of my bacon wrinkles until then."

If you are thinking of happy times from the past, these could cause sadness and unhappiness with the present.
"My period in college was fantastic. I made a lot of friends, lots of time to myself and had no wrinkles. It's unlikely to ever again look this gorgeous."

There's nothing more important in life than letting go of the things that made us pain and became the reason we failed. Learn from your mistakes get up and keep moving forward with a steady speed and do not forget to take pleasure in the journey to reach your goal.

Future-oriented living
Another location that is frequently preferred in comparison to "living in the present" is to think about the future. The constant thought of the future causes anxiety as well as anxiety,

discontent and tension.

"I must go to the store to buy some groceries. I also did not make an appointment with the doctor. I must write an assignment for work. I'm so overwhelmed!"

Instead of taking an afternoon stroll in natural surroundings, you fill your mind with thoughts such as: "Oh no, when I return back home, I need to wash your laundry and water my gardens after which the day will be over. I'm also supposed to get up earlier as Monday is an extremely labor-intensive day at work."

It's worse when you are in control from weekday to weekend. As if the days you have free were all the day on which you could live your life happily. Many people keep track of the days until their holidays throughout the year:

"I am so excited to lay on the beach of the Caribbean and sip my margarita in my hammock. Unfortunately, until then I'm living in cold Germany with re-gene-like weather and a lot of anxiety."

The idea of a perpetual life in the future drags you down. This prevents you from being present and enjoying the positive aspects of your life today.

A cost-effective, but most importantly positive and constructive outlook on the future is normal and is definitely important to keep your life enjoyable and prosperous. Future-oriented thoughts help us to make plans for the next steps of our lives. Yet, all too often, we use our energy and time to worry about the untrue aspects of the future.

Take a look at yourself for a day and you'll see that a substantial portion of your vision of the future is based on thoughts that can have an adverse effect on your wellbeing as a result of anxiety of insecurity, anxiety, stress or discomfort.

Words have power.
The average American spends about half his day with himself through thoughts. The bulk

of this inner dialogue is comprised of answers and questions. If we are confronted with situations that require our response when we review the proposal of someone to us, or if we try to determine the root cause of a fall is causing us pain, or we experience physical pain, our brain will analyze the situation by asking one of the following inquiries: What's taking place to me? How can I respond, and what should I do? Whatever circumstance you're in the three questions above seem to be the method your brain is trying to figure out the situation:

What's the matter? What's the problem? What can I do? For the answer to the questions above, you brain is simply searching the archives of your unconscious mind to find the most exact answer that is based on the knowledge and experiences you find in the files.

If you are able to ask yourself "Why is everything going so wrong in my life?" following a serious fall, even if it's an insignificant fall, as in our case your brain will look for an solution.

The first thing your brain will be able to discern is that your account isn't a true evaluation based on your past experiences, as not every thing you've attempted during your time has been successful. If there is no real evidence to back up the exaggeration you have incorporated into the question Your brain will look for additional information stored in your subconscious. It will consider all you've learned from other people regarding falls. Your own words and read, or seen on television or read about Based on this vast amount of data, whether accurate or incorrect either real or fictional You will be able to get an answer. Maybe you will find the answer to be "This happens to you because you're a scumbag!

It's not easy to pinpoint the source of this information. Perhaps it was a comment you made after falling or perhaps you read the statement in the circle of acquaintants or friends or have it appear in your morning horoscope. Whatever the source of that quote the real response is that it causes you to feel more miserable than you did before. It's simple: if one asks an insanity-inducing question, you'll definitely receive a sloppy answer.

The Law of Attraction clearly states that the reason behind negative emotions and negative feelings finding the answer is because you have asked the wrong question. Consider, for instance, thinking briefly about the following issues that lots of individuals ask themselves a surprising frequency:

What is the reason this occur to me?
- What makes it so difficult to master something?
- Why isn't money enough?
Why am I not so lucky?
- Why do I get fat so quickly?

What are the implications of these questions for your outlook? Be aware that your emotions and the quality of your life are influenced by the quality of the questions that are asked.

For instance, if you think: "Why do I get fat so fast? " It is likely that you're in a position to go on the same way you asked it, and your brain will store the information. The most likely answer you'll give yourself to this type of inquiry would be "You have a lot of fat, and you're fat due to the fact that you consume food all day long and you have no influence over your diet".

How does this response you have given your mind you? Do you feel more or less? Does this give you an answer to your issue? Do you find it helpful to bring the issue under control or, in the opposite do you feel unable? What's wrong with this statement is that it suggests that you are overweight. It is not the conditions which cause you to become fat and that it is normal for you to become fat fast.

If you're looking to shed weight, you must consider the following questions: "What can I do to lose weight and reach the ideal body weight? Do you see the differences? Furthermore, you can go one step more and

add:
"What do I need to do in order to shed some weight and attain the ideal body weight? What should I do today? How can I achieve it? I can be able to enjoy losing weight?
This implies that it is not only possible to reach your target, but it's also possible to be able to enjoy the journey to get there. You declare your commitment and request clear suggestions which you can immediately implement.

Do you see the significant differences in how your question is answered? It's much more effective when you ask questions that are positive since you will receive more positive responses. Be sure that your queries are specific to locating the resources already present in your life and will help you overcome any problem you encounter.

The potential of autosuggestions
To demonstrate the power of suggestion, I'll tell you about an experiment you are invited to test yourself.
Request a person to stretch their arms to the side and hold them as stiff as you can in this posture. Then , try pushing the arms back. If you are able to overcome some challenges, you can be successful.

Then ask the person to repeat the negative phrases for about a minute"I am ugly! I'm a loser! I'm dumb! I'm not enough! I am weak! I'm not able to do that! Then ask them to hold their arms stretched and stiff again before moving them back up. You'll notice that this time , you will need to exert less force to push your arms back down.

It took only just thirty seconds worth of defiant messages to alter this young man's self-esteem to the amount that he lost physical power. It is well-known that negative comments can affect the posture of a person and their condition but you'll be shocked by what these negative statements can do to your body's energy levels.

Man is a believer in anything that is repeated regardless of whether it is a truthful or false claim. If a lie is repeated for long enough and is accepted as truth as time passes. The mind will eventually accept it as a lie and will behave according to the new reality created by it.

What do you think of this knowledge? Begin by replacing the negative statements you have used so far, to positive statements that evoke the desired outcomes. Formulate them as if they were taking place or are likely to happen within the next few days. Be aware that in the present you have everything that you need to be successful. It is important to believe in that as well. It is the only way to harness the power that is stored in your subconscious to focus your thoughts on the path to success, and to reprogram them in the fullest meaning of the word. If you're seriously seeking out ways to utilize the "programming feature" The following steps will guide you to alter your inner dialogue:

1. It's a good idea to go over some of the words that you frequently use and especially those that limit and weaken your. Make a note of them and go through them several times. Take a look at each statement and think about whether they will benefit you or harm you. Consider if they can aid in building your self-esteem or make you feel less confident as an individual.

2. Discover the reasons you got started. What was the process that made these thoughts part of your internal conversation? Who brought them into your attention? What led you to feel this way? You'll be shocked by that how absurd a lot of these notions that limit us come to your mind. Maybe it was a fellow student in school who you liked who said you were ineffective and you've lived with the

idea that was hidden in your mind. It's possible that the same person you admire today isn't your friend anymore or a person with a problem who's been unable to find an employment for longer than six months after graduation and hasn't had much success in her life. Yet, in a strange way, you still hold the opinion of your mind and have accepted it as the truth.

Imagine what could be the outcome If Albert Einstein had listened to the doctor who identified him as mentally retarded due to his apparent difficulties in formulating words, or when the teacher who had criticized him for his frequent absence from class, suggested to his parents expel him from the school as he could be distracting the students who were not there regardless. There is no one who can remember the names of or the accomplishments of these two individuals however, we know that Albert Einstein was and what his contributions to the realm of science. If someone is going to criticize your capabilities, don't accept it without considering the legitimacy or validity of their criticism. Instead. We are usually criticized by those who are entitled to get criticized for this particular issue. The people who criticize themselves project shortcomings onto their surroundings.

Chapter 9: Ways to Make Universe Work for You Using the Law of Attraction

The law of attraction is dependent on your reaction to it. You can use it to be beneficial for yourself by using various methods to attract things that perform for your benefit. There are a few practical strategies that you can employ that are effective. There are many ways that might work for you but others may not. Therefore, look into different ways and then try the most effective for yourself.

1. Be thankful

The first thing you must do is to be thankful. Be grateful for the relationships that you have as well as the things you have and the love you receive from your spouse and family. When the universe recognizes that you're thankful, positive energy attracts you to it by itself.
You can keep a journal in which you are able to note all the positive things you're grateful for.

2. Make use of the Focus Wheel

The focus wheel is ways to remain true to your law of attraction. It helps you attract the beliefs that you want to attract and creates change in your life. Your behavior will change by itself thanks to the focus wheel.

3. Dream Board

Create a dream board for your bedroom. If you want to keep it private , it's yours to decide. You are able to draw images on it of what you would like to include. Record your goal on it. This will allow you to visualize the goal or dream that you would like to accomplish within your own life. If you see it every day it will remind you of your goal and will be in your head all time.

4. Visualize

Imagine your ideal dream and the parts that make it. For instance, if you want to visit a place that you are passionate about, imagine the location in your mind. Consider the places you'd like to visit. Focus on the smallest things and your feelings about it.

5. Affirmations

Affirmations are extremely powerful in the

realm of attraction. Write a sentence that you can think of and repeat frequently to yourself. For example , you can say "life is improving", "it will get better". The more often you repeat that, the more powerful it will be , and it will prevent you from negative thoughts.

6. Entertainment for brainwaves

Explore the brainwave game that keeps you focused on your mind by the ability to bring your dreams to life. It increases awareness and has a an immense influence on your daily life. You can download the brainwave audio files and listen whenever you want to reap the benefits.

7. Goal Setting

It is crucial to establish an objective to be able to work towards it. Once you have a clear idea of what you are trying to accomplish then you can organize the activities necessary to get there in the right time. The goal will be established and all tasks will be completed in accordance with it.

8. Talk

Speak to a trusted person about your dreams. Someone you be sure don't divulge any details about you to anyone else. It will communicate to the universe of what you want and will help to attract the universe towards you.

9. EFT (Emotional Freedom Techniques)

The technique can be utilized to think about what you want to achieve. Simply tap your fingertips on the table or on the desk wherever you're sitting. It assists you in focusing and increase the speed by putting pressure on your fingertips.

10. Audio Books

Audiobooks are the most effective ways to increase the motivation you need to accomplish your goals. Listen to whatever you like, and it's accessible at no cost. Browse the web and you'll find something that you'd like to hear.

11. Point of intent

Intention Point is also known as meeting place too. It is the place where you meet between your heart and your mind. You must find a the right balance for both to be steady in your daily life. If both are in a stable and solid connection, your energy is high and you can react normal to situations. The strong connection between brain and heart ensures that the universe knows you are always listened to and that you are granted the desire that you've always wanted.

12. Live life "as as".

Accept the reality and live with the reality. When we are in an issue and we want to be hidden and do not want anyone to notice us. Why is this? You must be able to live now because this moment is not going to come back. Spend some time shopping and enjoy your time, not just wasting your time. Enjoy a night out with companions and have fun. Even if you're worried it won't be a alter if you're worried. What's the point to worry about? It is simply to give it to the universe for good and have fun with your life. Take every moment in the present because they aren't coming back. Every breath you take is going to go out of your body and if it seems like you're taking it for nothing, it indicates that you're not thankful and is a sign of displeasure to the universe to not to be able to react to your needs.

13. Spread Positivity

Do not believe in yourself only for yourself, but spread the positivity around. At home or with your family or your spouse, or any other person who is around you. You can guide them in the best way you can to help them find the positive aspects of life. Let them see the light in life, and let them know that everything will be okay and that they will get it all back in the end. When you are stressed in your brain, nothing can help but it can affect your overall health. Don't complain too much, instead remain content with the present of world. You're getting the things you deserve and are likely to get more when you remain positive , because the universe never plays fair to any person.

14. Be Kind and Act in Kindness

If you can help someone and they're in need of it the right way, you must be the first to assist. There's not a lot of occasion that someone needs you , so if you are given the an opportunity to help, do not take it for granted. Don't think to think they didn't help you, but instead be kind and helpful for no reason. It sends an indication of gratitude and they'll surely appreciate your work more than they did previously. Every good thing you do will be added to the list of the universe. Even if you don't remember, you'll be blessed somehow somewhere in your life that you could never have imagined.

15. Read Quotes

Check out the inspirational quotes online and trust these quotes. They are written by individuals who have observed the reality of life too tightly. They believe in that law and have a clear understanding of the truth behind it. The people of the past were wiser and were able to think about their lives better than people of our generation. Take their advice and follow it. Check out motivational quotes from famous people because they have an eye for the success and the failures. There have been many changes and ups because of the fact that they have reached the top of their game throughout the world. If anyone knows about the person, then they know there is a lot of effort behind this person's success. in that position.

16. Let it go

Let go of the circumstances that can cause negativity in your mind. Let the universe do what it wants to and not interfere. There is no need to respond with anger or frustration as it is not going to do anything but affect your attitude and behavior. Therefore, let it go and let it be. It is not necessary to complain or regret about the situation since there's no purpose of it.

17. Make an agenda of your wishes

Everybody has wishes in their lives, regardless of how wealthy or poor. Whatever you have, no matter how much you own, you'll desire something more. Everyone has something or the other, but when they see another person wants it, they want it as well. It's an aspect of human nature, however, if you truly want to reach to a goal, write it down. Write it down and keep working on it. Maintain a positive mindset and go through the list. Write down your wishes according to priority. Once you have it, cross it. It sends a message your universe to let them know that you want it, and if you're working towards it, it will help you reach it. It offers possibilities to you that you've not ever imagined. If you are feeling that your relationship is getting worse than it was before, write it down first, and then do all possible things you could to make it better. If it doesn't let it go, leave it to the universe and it will perform all the miracles that will leave you satisfied and content to go on to the next one.

18. Do not believe in a limited view

The truth of a belief is not only half-hearted or limited. Therefore, ensure that you trust in the universe. It is not possible to act with fear and then sit comfortably and contemplate the fact that you believe in. You must act on it regularly. If you've decided on the destination you must go, then put your faith in the universe that it will definitely help you get there regardless of whether anyone would like it or not. If something is intended to be yours it will definitely be there for you regardless of what. Therefore, you must be confident about the outcome and strive to achieve it with optimism. Don't be afraid to feel unsecure since it only causes more chaos in your mind for no reason. Eliminate the negatives out of your life and begin to think with all your heart that you want to do the best.

As you continue to practice these techniques the more the universe will work in your favor. It is not necessary to write down every one of them, but pick one or two that be the most effective for you. It may be different for anyone as each person has different types of personality. For that law of attraction to be effective to your advantage, everybody has to be able to demonstrate the same behavior. You only need to be positive with complete faith in the universe to always be working for you to the best of your ability. Everyone wants to be content and knowing the concept of law of attraction can help you achieve happiness in a more simple method. A few simple guidelines are all you need to follow and life can unfold as you imagine it will be, with the comfort and ease.

Chapter 10: Visual Thinking: Step by Step instructions for Programming Your Mind to make more money, gain power and Respect

Making a Strong Intention

To program your mind to attract greater power, money as well as respect for others, you need set an empowering intention. An intention is basically a thought from a higher-consciousness. The difference between a standard thought and an intent is due to the fact that typical thought is more focused on an outcome that is specific, whereas an intention is the desire to be not restricted to a particular result.

If you make an request to the universe you are allowing the universe to come up with the best answer or result. Also you're not asking for something that is specific. A goal is all about creating a set of guidelines for the desired outcome, not seeking something that is that is too specific. Sometimes, our minds are too literal or narrow in regards with thinking about the Law of Attraction. It's easy to get habitually thinking in a certain way that it becomes difficult to think more expansively. Setting an intention can help to expand your thinking.

The universe operates within the field of energy that is infinite So putting some criteria around something you would like and wish for just limits your thoughts aren't unlimited. You aren't able to see the bigger picture but the universe could! The power of intentions is immense and is a lot of enjoyment to send something into the universe without knowing how it will be returned.

A desire must be fueled with faith and be able to believe with all your mind and heart that your wish will be granted in some way, manner or shape. Sometimes, it's not necessary to determine how the task will be fulfilled, since it only hinders your ability to think. In reality, there are millions of possibilities for the universe to make your dreams come true which is half the excitement!

The intention of your mind directs your attention to an entirely new direction, allowing you to create your own reality. Let's say that you are in search of a new position. You may think it's quite rational to express the idea of "getting an opportunity to work in a higher-paying job". But, this could restrict you since in putting forth the idea of obtaining the best job, you're reducing the likelihood out any chance that your current job will change in any way. A more effective goal could consist of something such as: "My next job is thrilling that makes me smile and is a natural flow for me, and I'm able to develop and learn from it". This will open you up to opportunities you might not have thought of before.

Let's review a few fundamental rules to follow in the process of making powerful goals. In essence, an intention is calling out a desire, without limiting your choices on how it should be expressed.

How to Create a Powerful Intention

* Decide to shift your perspective and expand your mind.

• Forget about your mistakes and learn not to dwell on it.

* Consider what you really want into your soul.
Don't limit yourself. Try to look at the bigger overall
* Make a choice to be content and to be gentle with yourself.
* Determine who you want to be and not what you'd like to be.
* Write down your intentions and repeat it over and over again.
* Keep an eye on your thoughts!
• Watch your words, and eliminate words such as should or never.
Stop blaming yourself for your life and begin acting instead.
* Work with a partner and make plans together, and make sure that you both are accountable.
Concentrate on the mindset or the condition you're striving to achieve and not on the mindset that you're moving away from.
In order to set powerful intentions, you must abandon your old habits of mind. It is time to be able to stop defying yourself with other terms. Sometimes, we're the worst of

ourselves because we are often very harsh on ourselves.

If you are able to put aside all limitations and focus on what it is that you truly desire in your heart, you'll set a strong intention. When making intentions it is important to put aside the past since it's over and done with and you won't be able to return. Remind yourself that you did the very best job with the information and knowledge you had at the time , and take a step forward.

It's time to think of more ambitiously about your life, because the fact of the thing is that you'll achieve everything.

If you determine the person you'd like to be are aligned with your values and goals and you begin doing your daily activities with greater enthusiasm and meaning. You have to decide to be happy whatever it is, by putting yourself in the top position. When you get rid of negative self-talk, it will alter your thoughts since you're no longer self-defeating.

You can be sure that you'll soon step into a more fulfilling life. Everything you have in your life exists because you intend it to be there. If you're looking to build better and more fulfilling life, then you need to create better goals and be confident that they will manifest regardless of what.

Setting a strong intention - A method for change

1. Concentrate on the part of your life that you would like to change Doing too many issues at once disperses your energy.

2. Be confident in yourself and know that it is possible to change your life through faith.

3. Start forming your goal within your head, taking away any notions of limits.

4. Allow the plan to manifest by appearing as if you've placed an order and are looking forward to it be delivered.

5. Prepare for the unexpected. Create your list of all the possibilities of how your plan could be realized.

6. Try to form your idea in a general manner , and do not be too specific. You must allow the universe some freedom in this instance.

7. Seek out clues to show up Don't be swayed by your intuition , or any synchronicities you may experience. This is the way for the

universe to let you know that your intentions have been heard!

8. Set your goals for the day as you go through the days!

Your goals are extremely strong and the only limitations you're faced with are the notions that you've set in place. It is essential to let your mind open and think about what you would like to be, not what you'd like to be. Enjoy the feeling that you feel when you imagine you living your life to the fullest and a life that is in sync with your goals.

Note down as many things that you can think of that you're thankful for, both things that you already have and the things you imagined being offered to you.

Step-by-Step directions to program your Mind to Increase Money and Power. and Respect

The most successful people around the globe have relied on the power of imagination and visualization to accomplish their goals and you can too. The majority of the time, our minds are cluttered. We're used to jumping between tasks to keep up with the latest happenings and so the notion of having a single focus point concentration may be difficult for those of you.

There are numerous ways to focus on a single point of focus, such as meditation as well as guided imagery and hypnosis however for the purposes of this book , we'll concentrate on the basic tools of imagination and visualization since they are simple to use. Napoleon Hill referred to the imagination as the "workshop of the mind" in his bestselling workbook, Think and Grow Rich. We don't often make use of this technique in our everyday lives, but the truth could help envision your goal more precisely.

If you want to point your brain in a new direction, there's nothing better than imagination.

The Law of Attraction is an abstract idea. In order to make it perform, you must make a powerful statement, and then focus the direction of that goal.

Bring that passion together with your imagination and creativity You can turn into

an enacting machine. The best method to concentrate your thoughts is to be absolutely clear on the things you'd like to achieve. Once you are specific about what you are looking for it is then possible to utilize the tools of visualisation and imagination to direct your thoughts towards the correct direction.
When you are at this point on your journey, you need to take a moment and think about what it is that you are truly looking for. When you're contemplating what you'd like to achieve, ensure that it's something you truly desire and really want. Also, make sure it's something that can enhance your life in a meaningful way.
What are you looking for?
Check Your Top Fundamental Values
In examining power, money, and respect, you need to ask yourself, what would your life be like if you had achieved all of these objectives? What does money mean to you? What is power to you? What would your life look like different if you were to be treated with more respect? Create a powerful idea with these thoughts in the mind.

If you're finding it difficult to decide what you want to do first, try selecting the one that will have the greatest impact in the event that it happened or occurred.

It can be difficult to imagine making a change to all of the things, but it's easy to think of making changes to one element that is crucial. Imagine this for the "tipping tipping point".

Make the assumption that if this single element changed, everything else would follow in accordance with the principle of the domino effect.

This aspect of the exercise is very crucial, so you should spend all the time you'd like playing around with various ideas and goals. You might think that you already have an idea of what you're after, but give yourself enough time to be more specific about it.

Here are some of the questions you should think about:

1. What can you do to feel strong?
2. What can you do to feel more valued?
3. What can you do to feel prosperous and abundant?

4. What makes you feel most strongly?

5. What makes you feel the most confident? There are many things present in your life, or that you are still trying to accomplish or attain. In the case of respect, power, and money make sure you don't get too specific, as you don't want limit your self to just one aspect. The universe could have something different in mind for you, therefore if you focus your attention on the emotions which money, strength and respect bring the feeling, you'll be better able to be open to any the universe decides to bless you with these things.

Let's look at some step-by-step instructions for you to aid in this process of visual thinking.

Step One - Clear your mind.

This is clearly easier to do than said. It doesn't require an expert in meditation to achieve. You can get rid of your mind in just a 5 minutes of meditation. Don't be at all intimidated by this part of the process. Only a calm mind can produce a clear view and this is a crucial step. Understanding how to listen to the silence that is within is the primary step. If you're having difficulty in calming your mind listen to gentle music or ambient tones like ocean waves or the soft rain. Many smart phones come with meditation apps that come with free ambient sounds, and they are great to work with. The practice of meditation or simply quieting your mind can have many benefits for health Set the timer, and then practice using different sounds until you discover one that's relaxing and pleasing to you.

Step 2 - Try practicing with an easy task, like imagining what you would like to do in your life.

Take a moment to close your eyes, and then take couple of deep breathes. In your mind's eye imagine yourself enjoying a fantastic day. If you're looking for more power, money, and respect, imagine yourself at your workplace or at a place you feel valued.

Imagine what your ideal day looks like. Pay attention to the little particulars. Imagine yourself getting dressed for the day and then doing your daily routine. Visualize exactly what your house or the environment is like , right down to the smallest point. Sit down with a cup coffee or tea and take a seat in your living space and observe, feel or feel the objects that surround you.

Take note of the textures, shades and how the house is like. Imagine your self getting dressed for work and think about what type of car you use. Get in the car and take a drive. Imagine yourself getting to your workplace or wherever you are going and imagine what people will think of you. Consider yourself to be a powerful person who is worthy of respect.

Practice until you've got clear vision in your mind's eye the perfect day.

Step Three: Practice with something more challenging in your practice and make a commitment to regular routine.

Do it on a greater scale right now. Make a commitment to yourself to block out 5-10 minutes each day (more depending on how you feel about it) to focus and practice controlling your thoughts. Making a habit of making time for this is essential to your success with practicing the Law of Attraction. Don't make the mistake of thinking you're not capable of doing it as everyone has the same amount of time in a day. If you're having difficulty finding time, take the time in the shower to give an example or even your journey to work, if you take buses or trains. It is possible that you are unable to shut your eyes, but you'll still be able to daydream and let your thoughts wander.

If you have an afternoon break, you can take 5 minutes of your schedule to relax and imagine. Make use of a device like walking meditation when you enjoy being active and focused. Incorporate this practice into your every day routine and you'll be eagerly anticipating your short breaks as the best part in your daily routine.

Focus on the items you're hoping to incorporate in your own life. You can focus on an upgrade to your car, a new home, a brand new method to earn money or even an enjoyable and healthy relationship. If you're trying for ways to boost your fitness, think on how you'd feel to be healthier. Imagine yourself moving around effortlessly and enjoying time with family and friends for instance. The beach is an excellent location to imagine your health and wellness, as it is easy to imagine you running around and playing at the shoreline.

If you're than a little spiritual you can imagine sitting somewhere sacred or private like a gorgeous lake or gazebo , and having a chat with an angel or a spiritual counselor of some sort. This could represent an angel spiritual guide, priest or priest, or God. Your mind is unlimited therefore

Go to wherever you'd like to go with this exercise.

Do at least 5-10 minutes per day then in no time you'll be doing between 20 and 30 minutes without any issue whatsoever. Don't be stressed out about trying to go for longer and longer durations of time, if you don't be able to do it try to work it out gradually and it will become simpler and easier.

Chapter 11: Power of Mindfulness Meditation

Focusing and meditating for a set amount of time, also called meditation, is deep in the ancient civilizations and is practiced by religions and cultures from across the globe. The first evidence of meditation's existence, which we haveis wall artifacts dating from the Indus Valley dating between 3500 and 5,000 BCE. They show people sitting on the ground, with their hands placed on their knees and with their legs crossed. It is a position that is widely regarded as the most popular form of meditation.

The ancient Indian texts have provided us with methods of meditation that date back to more than three thousand years long ago. Today, meditation isn't just for the purpose of religion but it is also the principal tool used by people to relax their minds and create a sense of relaxation and peace. There are many types of meditation as it's used in many forms and, if you're a novice who wants to reap these benefits, here you'll find a listing of the most commonly used meditation styles:

* Transcendental Meditation A simple method of meditation in which a personal selected mantra, typically an energizing and familiar phrase or word, repeats in a certain manner.

* Mindfulness Meditation This is the practice by which you are completely present and at peace with your thoughts and not involving your thoughts about everything going in the world around you.

*Mantra Meditation: The method of meditation includes mantras, which are calming phrase or word to stop the person not to be distracted by thoughts while contemplating.

* Vipassana Meditation The Vipassana Meditation is an old Indian type of meditation in which you observe things in the way they are. It is the definition that is associated with Vipassana is the Sanskrit phrase Vipassana.

* Guided Meditation This is a technique by which you can visualize scenarios or mental images that calm you.

* Loving-Kindness Meditation: Also known

under the name Metta practice, this method lets you focus your love and kindness to others.

* Meditation through Yoga: It is an additional traditional Indian practice that requires you to practice a variety of postures and breathing exercises designed to increase the peace of your mind and increase flexibility.

* Chakra Meditation It is a series of exercises for relaxation that concentrate on healing and the chakras to bring balance and spiritual strength for your physical body.

Meditation can provide many benefits that are well-known even within researchers. For example, if you practice regular meditation, you'll notice a significant reduction in stress that is among the primary reasons people decide meditation in the beginning. In general, mental and physical stress can lead to an increase of cortisol which is the stress hormone. This hormone triggers the numerous negative consequences of stress like disturbance of sleep depression, anxiety and elevated blood pressure and fatigue. Meditation can also help reduce stress, as less stress means less anxiety. It can also help reduce symptoms of anxiety disorders, such as social anxiety fears, phobias, paranoid thinking as well as panic attacks and obsessive-compulsive behavior. It is also possible to ensure that your emotional health is maintained at an optimal levels through various forms of meditation. They could lead to an optimistic perspective on life, and improved self-esteem and confidence. Meditation with mindfulness is usually recommended to those who are looking to build and maintain their emotional well-being.

A greater awareness of yourself is another benefit you'll experience when you practice regular meditation as it will aid in understanding your own self better and assist you in becoming the best version of yourself. For instance, self-inquiry mediation can help you to understand yourself better, but also how you're associated with the people who surround you. There are different types of meditation that allow you to discern the various thoughts that could be harmful and self-defeating by becoming aware of the pattern of your thoughts. If your thoughts start to turn negative, you'll be able to figure out how to redirect them toward more positive avenues.

Meditation practitioners who practice focus-focused meditation report increasing the duration of their focus. This type of meditation increases your focus and strengthens it by enhancing capacity of focus. Even meditating for just a short duration can be extremely beneficial to increase your ability to focus. A study for instance found it takes four days to complete practice is sufficient.

There are also reports that meditation could help aid in reducing memory loss that occurs due to the aging process. As we've mentioned that meditation increases the clarity of our thinking and focus, two elements that can aid in keeping your mind fresh despite physical age. The method of meditation known as Kirtan Kriya incorporates the chanting or mantra, and the constant movement of fingers to concentrate thoughts. Meditation has also produced promising results for improving memory problems, especially for people suffering from dementia.

It is a virtue that can be taught by practicing meditation. Different types of meditation can increase positive behavior towards yourself and others and positive emotions. For instance the meditation of loving kindness, or Metta as we have previously discussed begins with the development of positive thoughts and feelings towards yourself. As you continue to practice you will learn to extend the forgiveness and kindness you show to new acquaintances, first friends and, at the end even to those you don't like.

Meditation is recommended to those who are suffering from addiction behavior. This is due to the fact that when you complete a practice of meditation you have to build your mental discipline. As the result, it will aid in breaking the cycle of dependency by increasing your awareness, control of your behavior and help you comprehend what triggers these addictive behavior. According to studies, meditation can aid many people in understanding how they can refocus their attention to increase their willpower, be aware of the reasons behind their addictions and manage their urges, such as cravings for food, and even their moods.

Many suffer from or be affected by insomnia at one point or another in their lives. Meditation and mindfulness can assist in improving sleep by redirecting your mind's erratic thoughts that tend to be the root of insomnia. It helps to ease your body into relaxation and put your body in a relaxed state through the release of tension. In turn, you're more likely to sleep. Similar to this meditation can help control discomfort since the perception of pain is dependent on the state of mind that can be improved in stressful circumstances. Through meditation, you'll experience pain but not as much, but you'll gain an increased capacity to deal with it, and perhaps even feel an easing of pain.

These benefits of meditation which are supported by scientific research aren't only worth the time spent in meditation but should inspire you to begin meditating. Based on the benefits mentioned above meditation can assist you in fight off diseases.

Mindfulness meditation , also called therapeutic meditation, is a technique which is designed to increase your focus and mental relaxation. The term mindfulness refers to an approach that has been practiced over a long period of time, and is often referred to for its transcendental meditation. Its roots are traced to India and more specifically the Vedic tradition. It is closely linked to the yoga system as well as Ayurvedic medicine. Meditation principles can be found within Qigong, Tai Chi, breathing regulation, as well as the relaxation response.

For many years, the practice of meditation was thought to be the best way to overcome all the problems of life. But, it's more about the ability to enjoy peace in your mind. However, this is just a small portion of the practice of meditation, and many aren't in a position to attain this through just a few minutes of daily practice. This specific misconception kept meditation off the radar for quite a while as it did not resolve all problems as some believed. Today, however it is practiced daily by millions of people with an unambiguous goal that has the most beneficial for health. The definition of mindfulness is as a way of observing what happens to every moment of your life regardless of whether the experiences are challenging, painful or simple.

The benefits in mindfulness have been researched and debated by a variety of scientists due to the fact that it is not fully understood how it could have remarkable results on wellbeing of the body. We know that changing our mental state can have powerful benefits. For instance this phenomenon of placebo has proven its healing abilities without the use of medication or a medication. What it helped in establishing notion was the fact that it was an intervention. One of the many studies of the placebo effect utilized the participants in a group and directed them to take the pills that contained the active ingredient. The other group received the sugar pill. The two groups did not know which pills they received. The placebo was found to provide different benefits for people who believed they were taking it, whereas the other group only took a sugar pill. The phenomenon has been a mystery to researchers and is due to the fact that brains are a complex organ , and meditation can have many advantages for healing.

Neuroscience has begun to determine how meditation affects humans' brains. One study studied the brain's activity using the use of magnetic resonance (MR) prior to and following the practice of meditation and within the time frame of eight weeks. It was found that the University of Massachusetts found in the study "Mindfulness practice results in increases in gray matter density in the region of the brain. density" by Britta K. Holzelab James Carmody, Mark Vangel, Christina Congleton, Sita M. the Yerramsettia Tim Gard, and Sara W.Lazara this:

A study of these images showed the decrease in the density of grey matter in the brain. Particularly they measured the changes in the hippocampus that is believed to be vital for learning and memory as well as being connected to compassion, introspection and self-awareness.

* They also saw in the pictures a decrease in density in other brain regions.
* The amygdala that is a key player in anxiety and stress decreased of grey matter.

The research has also been conducted to determine the long-term effects that healing meditation can have in the mind. The study was conducted during 2012, by Gaelle Desbordes T. Lobsang Negi, W. Thaddeus, W. Pace, B. Alan Wallace, Charles L. Raison along with Eric L. Schwartz, utilized the technique of functional magnetic resonance (fMRI) to examine precisely this. Researchers discovered:

* Increases in brain activity within the amygdala.
* Brain activity changes for people who remained the same in the absence of meditation.

It was concluded that meditation may lead to learning that is not particular to specific tasks, but rather specifically based on the brain's process. It can lead to lasting changes in the mental functioning. The most compelling evidence of healing meditation as shown by various researchers is treatment of anxiety and depression. Why? The practice of meditative for a long time could have long-term benefits in the capacity and performance that the brain of humans. The study was conducted with the involvement from Tibetan Buddhist monks, "Long-term meditaters self-induce high-amplitude, gamma synchrony while they are practicing their mental skills," by Antoine Lutz, Lawrence L. Greischar, Nancy B. Rawlings, Matthieu Ricard, and Richard J. Davidson, and it was found that they had an increase in the gamma signal throughout the human brain. Particularly:

* Meditation could boost the number of gamma waves that are present in the brain, which are the smallest forms of brain-based energy and are associated with feelings of gratitude.
* The monks displayed an enormous growth in gamma radiations that was that were not

seen before.

Other studies, for instance the "Hemodynamic responses of the prefrontal cortex in relation to attentional and meditation" conducted by Singh Deepeshwar, Suhas Ashok Vinchurkar Naveen Kalkuni Vishweswaraiah, as well as Hongasandra RamaRao Nagendra, have demonstrated that long-term practice of meditation as well as similar exercises for attention can boost the thickness and the blood flow to prefrontal cortex. This is the part that is associated with the ability to make decisions, influencing the personality and complex behaviour. For those who perform well, this is a vital functional part of the brain.

But, healing meditation goes beyond the functions and anatomy of the brain. The research conducted in the 1970s "A awake hypometabolic state of physiologic activity," by R. K. Wallace, H. Benson, and A. F. Wilson, found that meditation could alter the way that our bodies function. For instance, mindfulness may cause a state of 'hypo-metabolic which is like hibernation. When you achieve this state, the benefits can aid in improving the health and longevity of cells in our body. The intake of oxygen is reduced which leads to it entering an euphoric state. Today, our understanding of the gut microbiome of the human has allowed us to understand how this happens. Microbes in the trillions live in the digestive system , and they manage the gut lining as well as the immune system. It is well-known that stress can have a profound effect on the gut microbes. Meditation is a great aid in controlling the gut microbes' stress response through the replacement of chronic inflammation and the maintaining the gut barrier's health. The gut microbe does not only impact the immune system, but also gene expression. Based on various research studies like "What is the molecular signature for Mind Body Interventions? The Systematic Review Of Gene Expression Changes Induced by meditation and related practices" by Ivana Buric Miguel Farias, Jonathan Jong, Christopher Mee, and Inti A. Brazil, meditation can influence pro-inflammatory genes, which can in turn control inflammation. The effects are transmitted through the brain , and these genes were identified to boost the time it takes to respond for the brain's response to cortisol stress hormone, when they were tested by mental calculations and speaking before an audience.

Disorders like Type 2 diabetes, Alzheimer's disease, and other inflammatory digestive issues are linked by intestinal leakage. When stress hormones are lessen like cortisol and epinephrine by rest and relaxation along with mindfulness eating and meditation These tight junctions will be healed. Most neurotransmitters within your body get released via the microbiome of your gut. By meditating, we aid in controlling the stress response and reduce chronic inflammation, as well as maintain the gut barrier functioning in a healthy way.

The link between the gut and the brain is a key factor when we steal chronic digestive disorder. Because of this, the healing meditation to treat digestive disorders is supported by numerous studies like "Meditation and the effects of vacation" written conducted by E. S. Epel, E. Puterman, J. Lin, E. H. Blackburn, P. Y. Lum, N. D. Beckmann, J. Zhu, E. Lee, A. Gilbert, R. A. Rissman, R. E. Tanzi as well as E. E. Schadt. The study revealed that stress management strategies along with other psychological strategies, may aid those suffering from IBS. The results were extremely promising for at the very least a short time.

Based upon studies, chronic inflammation could result in a variety of chronic illnesses. A number of genetic genes get activated within the body by chronic inflammation. Intestinal permeability, or a leaky gut can be linked to numerous auto-immune, digestive and metabolic conditions that are all connected to inflammation. In the research study "What can be the Molecular Significance of Mind-Body Interventions? An Systematic Study of the Expression Variations Induced by meditation and other practices" composed of Ivana Buric Miguel Farias, Jonathan Jong, Christopher Mee, and Inti A. Brazil, has concluded that mindfulness may aid in the creation of opposite gene activation, which occurs in the context of inflammation.

What is the reason why mindful meditation or healing beneficial? The practice of mindfulness is to teach you to slow down the thoughts that race through your mind and body and let go of negative thoughts. In general, mindfulness practices differ however, they all include mindfulness of the body and mind as well as the practice. In mindfulness meditation it's not necessary to have essential oils or mantras or candles, except if you want to incorporate them into your routine. For you to begin practicing mindfulness meditation, all you require is about three or five minutes to clear your mind from judgments, as well as the ability to find a comfortable spot to sit.

Learning to meditate with mindfulness is easy to learn, however in the case of an intermediate level and need help, a teacher or program can help you begin, particularly in the case of meditation to improve your health. Be sure to take time to practice mindfulness even if you need to start your alarm one hour before when you typically wake up, but don't be overly burdened by your schedule as life can get busy sometimes Try again the next day.

The first step to meditation is finding a quiet and comfortable place to do your practice. You can choose to lie at the table or sit in the chair and keep your head, back and neck straight, but not stiff. It is also helpful by wearing loose, comfortable clothes to avoid being distracted. While it's not required, you could utilize a timer, or a gentle and gentle alarm to help to forget about time and concentrate on your medication , as well as eliminating any excuses that you might be able to use for stopping and doing something other.

Many people lose track the time when they meditate, and a timer, or an alarm can ensure that you're not in the habit of doing a lot of meditation. After your meditation time, allow yourself the time to rise slowly and be conscious of where you are. Pay attention to your breathing and feel the feeling of moving air that is moving through your body when you breathe. Be conscious of your belly sinking and rising when air flows through your nostrils before it exits your mouth. Concentrate your attention on the fact that every breath is unique and the way it is breathed changes. If you start to notice thoughts entering your mind , don't suppress these thoughts or deny them. Be calm and acknowledge them using your breath as a reference.

Chapter 12: What to Make Use of LOA to manifest various things

As we've seen The law of attraction says that we attract what we are focused on. So, whatever you decide to focus on, whether positive or negative the ability to manifest it is in you.

At first, implementing LOA in your life could appear to be a daunting task. Actually, it's not that difficult. The practice of LOA is boiled down to three basic principles: seek, believe and accept. For someone who's learned about the power of your subconscious mind for a long time I can say for certain that you utilize LOA everyday without even realizing.

Consider it this way. What number of times do you spent your nights dreaming for the following tomorrow would prove to be better one? What number of times put on your most loved piece of clothing to go for an interview, hoping that it will bring luck? Have you believed (hoping for some thing is as close as the concept of visualization as you can get) that something could happen but only to see it happen? I'd guess it was several times. The most common thing that we would like to call luck actually LOA that is guided by your vision and then realised in your mind's subconscious, with an enormous amount of help by the Universe.

As you can see, it is possible to make use of LOA to help you with nearly every pillar in your life. As with Howard Schultz, you can make use of it to create wealth. It is possible to use LOA to create whatever you want. If you want to have a stunning body, you can make it happen with LOA. If you want to have a great relationship is not a problem, just make use of LOA. LOA can be used for many purposes in daily lives.

Let's look at some ways you can make use of LOA to manifest different things in your life.

How to manifest Wealth and Abundance in 3 Easy Steps

Making use of LOA to create abundance and wealth is an option. However, one aspect I want to emphasize is that although it's in no way desirable for a person to live in poverty, it's equally true that greed doesn't lead to happiness.

To bring abundance and wealth into your life First thing to do is remove yourself from any subconscious or naive belief you might have regarding prosperity, money and wealth. Limiting beliefs are the largest factor in why many people utilize LOA but are unable to create prosperity or wealth in their lives. Consider that all that you see around you was in one way or another the thought of another and since you are the creator, master creator, and author of your universe There is no limit to the things you can create. Additionally, because we live in an enigmatized and vast world that is awash with possibilities, you are blessed with unlimited possibilities and resources if you make use of your mind.

In order to be prosperous It is essential to firmly hold the conviction that no one on earth is deficient. Everyone is born identical. It's only the beliefs we hold that limit our potential.

To create prosperity and wealth throughout your daily life follow this simple rule, the exact one Cynthia used to follow think and behave as though already have what you would like and it will be yours.

If you are able to manage this, it's the initial and fundamental stage to manifesting anything you would like to achieve. If this is already information in you, go through the following steps to manifest abundance and wealth.

First Step: Imagine and Feel It

Relax into a state of meditative and sit quietly, taking long breaths over a few moments. Your mind will be able to visualize your abundance and wealth. Do not just imagine it, sketch it out and embed it into your mind's subconscious. Imagine and feel what an exquisite home or a luxurious automobile, or money at the bank feels like. Consider and imagine how your life could be different. Take the time to feel the result. When you visualize, make sure to be concise. Do not just think about how money can affect your life. Consider how your money could affect the lives of the people in your life. What are the causes you would be willing to support? What would you do to help your family? What kind of business would you be operating?

Step 2. Believe

This is where a lot of people fall short. The problem is that they are unable to believe in themselves. It is an optimistic idea. We have already seen that to get LOA to be effective it is essential to nourish it with all the positive energy that you can attain. A desire to believe in contrast will create negative energies.

These two energies can't coexist. In order to manifest abundance and wealth it is crucial to believe that what you desire is yours or at minimum, is at your fingertips.

Step 3: Stay In Focus

As we've seen repeatedly that successful manifestation doesn't happen by chance. It takes consistent effort toward the realization of your dream. It requires determination and focus. The commitment to visualization, faith in the unlimited potential of our universe and to the idea that anything you want can be yours.

This commitment is the sole thing that will

guarantee that your vision is solid. A strong will is the only way to enforce your vision. The last step is the one that transcends all manifestations that is grateful receiving. Many of us have a conditioned belief that make us believe that we are not worthy. To be able to manifest abundance and wealth it is necessary to connect with God, and be open and willing to accept the notion that you too have the right to good experiences and things.

To make wealth manifest it is important to keep in mind that, before the universe can bring your attention to your desires it is essential to first experience and behave as wealthy. The secret to creating wealth is to lead an intentional life that is filled with joy and enthusiasm for your life and the experiences you have.

Utilizing LOA in order to Manifest Health and Wellness

It is also possible to use LOA to create wellbeing and health. In reality, as we've learned it is possible to use this law to bring about various things. While manifesting is based on the same fundamental tenet: seek, believe, and accept, manifesting different items can be different in their direction. In order to manifest your health or well-being Follow the steps below.

Step 1: Don't Concentrate on the Healing
The Law of Attraction is triggered by your thoughts of vibration. If you are using the law of attraction to bring abundance and health It is recommended to concentrate on health and health instead of focusing on healing. This is because thoughts that are constant towards healing center too much on the issue. This could reduce your creativity ability. Instead of looking at the healing process and all that you might have to do to recover concentrate on how amazing it will feel to be in good health. Concentrate on how wonderful you will be feeling once your recovery.

Step 2: Try thinking differently
In the midst of pain it's impossible to imagine or imagine that anyone else has gone through what you're experiencing and has won it. For instance, if you're suffering from cancer suffering and pain, it can make you believe

that it is impossible to fight. This shouldn't be the scenario.

Instead, you should attempt as many times as you can to view your circumstances through different eyes. For instance, looking at cancer through the eyes those who have overcome it can result in a positive placebo effect in your health overall. While looking at your current situation or your process with a different perspective is not going to alter your current circumstance or situation but it can provide you with an entirely new and fresh perspective from which to see the world. It allows you to appreciate your life in the way it is currently. With this appreciation and acceptance it is much more easy to achieve optimal health.

Step 3: Make use of affirmations

Daily affirmations can be used to achieve well-being and health. In this context an affirmation is the declaration of a promise of what you want. Positive health affirmations bring positivity and create an ideal conditions that allow attractivity to operate. To achieve optimal health, you can make use of affirmations like:

"I am healthy"

"My body is strong and healthy"

"My body and my life are filled with energy"

The process of manifestation is the same across all. Certain, manifestation of different aspects may require a modification of the fundamental process to ensure that it aligns in harmony with the life pillar you wish to enhance or alter however, the process of manifestation is the same. It is a matter of asking, believing and then accept it with gratitude.

Next chapter we will explore a few manifestation exercises that will help you to manifest what you'd like to.

Chapter 13: Law of Attraction Exercises

Shopping in the Whole Universe

Learn from your shopping habits at the supermarket. Note that if you shop at a supermarket without a listof items, you'll end up wandering through the aisles and putting things in your cart that you don't require. This is the same with this task. To gain access to and have what you are searching for all over the world it is necessary to create an outline of it. The list doesn't need to be written on paper. You are able to be as creative as desire. Write the list using sticky notepads which are hung in your bedroom. You can also create an image board that is not just words but also images of objects, people or events you wish to draw attention to.

One of the most effective shopping lists you can put together is a wish list. It's a diary, but instead of writing down every event that has occurred to you, opt to record only positive things. Create images or pieces of objects that you would like to draw attention to. It is best to keep the journal compact and easily portable so that you can carry it wherever. Be sure to affirm yourself by reading the words or pictures in this journal. You can also open it particularly when you're near to having negative thoughts enter your thoughts.

Additionally, your journal or whatever medium you choose to use doesn't have to be completed in one go. The list you create is an ongoing work. Always update it by adding entries that express your desires at any time during the day. Set a routine to look over or read your schedule at least once a every day. It should remind you of the ideas you are planning to create that will in turn bring you the things you'd like to accomplish.

It is not the list of names that make the Law become effective. The Law is based on your thoughts and the thoughts that it contains to draw the people you want. The list is merely an instrument to stimulate your mind to contemplate these thoughts. Each time you look at this list, you brain is filled with thoughts that are a reflection of the accomplishments on the list.

Making manifestations

The ability to manifest is among the most effective tools made available through the Law. Anyone who is able to master this technique are able to alter reality itself. It is the next step after a creative visualization, as well as the grocery list you've made. The process involves a mix of imagination and routine. Keep in mind that the Law states that your mind's ideas, when properly focused, can be used to alter or create our physical reality.

With your mind firmly focussed, bring them into reality. Believe that the thoughts you are thinking about can be occurring within the physical world. If, for instance, you wish to build profitable businesses, imagine yourself as the owner of this company. What do you do? What's your outfit? What's the balance in your account at the bank? How much revenue have you earned? How many customers are there in your shop? What items are the most popular? What do you think? What do you think?

Make sure you respond to these thoughts with affirmations. Don't let even a single sliver of doubt creep into your thoughts. Beware of the temptation to believe that these things can't occur or cannot be accomplished. Allow these thoughts to affect your actions and act, as well as your words. When you bring them in your own reality, you emit the energy that draws similar thoughts. This is the secret to manifestation. When you radiate energy that matches the pattern of energy that is similar to the thing you desire The thing will be drawn to your energy field.

Raising Frequencies

The most intricately connected idea of the Law and energy is frequency. The Law says that everything is in the universe, no matter how tangible, like your body, others objects, money events, or any other physical things , or intangible, like thoughts, ideas, feelings thoughts, feelings and many other things that are abstract are made of energy. Since everything is comprised out of energy various energies or frequencies and the energy produced by your thoughts is the pure and powerful.

It is so strong that the frequencies of human thought when in comparison to other frequencies of less important objects that all other objects or even the whole universe is trying to align to the greater frequency. Your thoughts are the basis to which all the universe's energies strive to be in sync with. Every other energy surrounding you will strive to align with your own energy. This means that your frequency will be amplified by the frequency that is corresponding to you. When you experience negative thoughts or lower frequency, the world of negativity will only attach onto you as directly in reaction to your negative thoughts.

To prevent this risk The best way to avoid this is to increase the frequency of your radio. There are two methods to increase it. One involves letting go, or let go of the things that reduce your frequency and are negatives that you experience in your life. Stress that is manageable and problems which can be addressed or concerns that you can tackle These are all aspects that are in your control. Let these thoughts and worries go, let them out of your mind and your thoughts.

Once you have eliminated these downers, it is now time to begin raising your frequencies. There are many methods you can employ to accomplish it. There are those who practice meditation and the technique that is deep breathing. It slows down heart rate, reduces blood pressure, and consequently creates peace and a relaxing feeling. When you are at peace You radiate powerful positive energy which can increase your energy levels.

Sleeping or resting is another option to increase the frequency of your brain. Sleep is like performing an easy reset to your frequency. This is extremely beneficial since humans are naturally tuned to a high frequency, and can only be reduced when it's weighed down by negative thoughts in the mind. When you go to sleep or take a rest the body goes through a process of relaxation, which leaves your mind ready to experience an increase in frequency once you awake.

In accordance with the laws, the best way to boost the frequency of your mind is to emit two essential thoughts: love and happiness. If these two thoughts are accomplished it is believed that your mind reaches the highest frequency. If you reach this kind of frequency you are the most effective and are able to access the maximum potential in using the Law. This exercise can be used in order to attract energies you believe are difficult or impossible to attain. The more engaged or more content you feel in your life, the more powerful your frequency and the more power you have to attract.

Other Exercises

In addition to the two exercises that are most effective that we have mentioned, you may utilize lesser but nevertheless crucial methods to entice those desires that are in your mind and heart. A few of the exercises you can practice daily include:

Appreciation: be grateful for all the things you see around you and especially the things you tend to overlook. The more you value your surroundings, the more you appreciate what you are blessed with within your own life. Instead of dwelling on things you don't possess, your focus will be on things you already have.

Courage: failures, problems and errors will occur. Instead of being overcome by them, build your strength to confront and overcome these issues. When you let fear take over your mind, it will just lower the frequency. But, if you've got the courage to face your fears and confidence, your mind will remain always in a state of positive energy, regardless of the efforts of negative thoughts to sway your thoughts.

Kindness: This exercise is essential in order to draw energy that is associated with individuals and their actions. If you wish to be a magnet for kindness you need to be kind to people around you. It's the same with compassion, honesty and love. You must radiate the qualities you wish to be able to receive.

Learning: open your eyes to new ideas, new lessons and other opportunities. Instead of allowing yourself to be restricted by your comfortable zones, broaden your horizons and gain knowledge rapidly. Be aware that experience might be the most effective teacher, but you still have the opportunity to learn important lessons from others who have been through the same process earlier than you.

Prioritize: The process of attracting the attention of those who have different things. Make sure you distinguish the ones you require from those you simply desire. Although the Law is applicable regardless of whether it's an actual need or desire When you meet your needs first, then the desires are sure to follow.

Chapter 14: Top Law of Attraction Myths debunked

Like every other popular notion that has gained traction, the law of attraction has drawn criticism as well as various myths that have developed as a result. Some people dismiss the concept because they've never been able to make use of the law in their lives. People tend to create beliefs about something due to the fact that they aren't aware of the process or are doing it wrong. Law of Attraction is effective in the real world, and if you follow the easy tips contained that are in the book you will be able to transform your life in a positive direction.

Here's the myths about the law of attraction and how they can be debunked:

Myth 1: This Don't Work for everyone

Another variation of this myth could be "the Law of Attraction did not apply to me." It doesn't matter if you have faith in or are aware of the law of attraction. It applies to all people. Every person creates their in the form of manifestation without even realizing it.

Even if you aren't creating the life you desire however, it's still taking place. The power lies in your power to use the law of your life and manage the manifestation. This is something everyone can master if they set their minds to it.

Background, race, age or even religion isn't a factor when implementing manifestation strategies properly. While some individuals might require more time and effort because of their beliefs and attitudes using the correct tools can make anyone a manifestation master. Here are some reasons why that the law of attraction might not work for you:

You always complain about everything that happens to you. It may be your husband or children and bosses, or your job. Every day you go to work and you walk into the day frustrated at, anxious, or dissatisfied.

You doubt your capability to manifest what you want. As you manifest your desires but you are adamant about contrary views

Relying on circumstances outside of your control to make you feel happy or content

* You're in a waiting state for something in

order to feel content. You could, for instance, have been waiting on a promotion to feel more successful, or awaiting to feel elated when you purchase a home or, even better, hoping to feel happy when you start an affair. But, relying on these situations to experience the way you want to feel can cause friction in your body's vibrations and you could be unable to achieve your objectives.

Myth #3: Need to Consider Something

The majority of people think that all you have to do to do to follow"attraction" is to to think about something and then will get it. The first time the novel "Secret" was first published in the early 1990s, a lot of people didn't know the concept or not know how it worked. The message has been passed through the years. Some people think that if you'd like an Rolls-Royce car all you have to be thinking about it continuously. Write your thoughts down, and you'll see it on your driveway. However, that's not exactly how law of attraction operates. The law doesn't respond to your thoughts , but your vibrations. Although it's partially true it is not enough engaging your law of attraction in order to buy an expensive Rolls-Royce model.

A couple of weeks ago, a customer said to me that he is unhappy when he sees the vision boards on his computer. Instead of feeling excited about the potential, he's discontent. The law of attraction is responding to the way he feels when the vision board. The board is drawing sadness.

The procedure is a straightforward one to ask the universe for what you would like believing, taking action, and then you will get it.

Ask the Universe

Focus your mind, keep thinking positive on the present moment, then ask your universe what you would like.

Believe

It is the point at which the majority of people end up. You believe you'll be able to achieve your goals and you do positive affirmations and journaling , as well as having vision boards, but then you put it all down. It is important to understand that believing is a part of being active. For instance, if you are aspiring to become an artist, you should enroll in the music program, and participate in auditions to further your career.

Receive

Prepare yourself to be filled with joy and gratitude being a part of the universe's offer to you. Although you might not get it right away, just be patient trust, be a believer, act and you'll be on the road to fulfilling your desires.

The Myth 3: Don't Need to Rethink Your Thoughts

It is said that the law of attraction can be achieved when you transform negative thoughts into positive ones and believe that you can achieve all you desire. Stop complaining about the things you can't get and replace negative thoughts with positive thoughts. Beware of thinking about that you don't like your job. Instead, think whether you can start your own company and imagine how great it will be to do what you enjoy doing.

Myth #4: No Action Required

Many people think that if they grab their bulls by the horns they're not actually applying this law. This is how the myth is dispelled. You won't just initiate the action, but you will also enjoy the process. Instead of taking a forced action like you're accustomed to, you'll substitute it with an inspiring action, one that you love and are happy performing it. A truly inspired action includes:

As a result of a job and you're excited about it
Feel your inner voice whispering to you, try this You've got this
* Feeling excited to get involved
Feeling well enough to continue to advancement and any action that comes next

Myth #4: Not Supposed to be

Another version of this legend one variation is "the universe is conspiring to harm you." This is not the case; the universe isn't working against anyone. Actually it will provide you with the food you feed it. If you're in a zone of judgment and resentment and resentment, that's what the universe will provide. If, on the other hand, you're in a space of joy and gratitude, your universe is sure to shower you with that.

Myth #6: A Terrible Event Happens Everytime You Negatively Think About It

The myth of this kind is prevalent in the world of people who are new to the law of attraction. In reality, at times negative thoughts can pop up in your mind. Physically, things don't appear immediately. There is a buffer period to shift your attention and thoughts to what you would like to achieve. We all would like to reach goals more quickly The buffer time helps by allowing us to shift negative thoughts. So, don't be anxious about negative thoughts that pop up randomly since once you have mastered your creative abilities and master the art of to change these thoughts.

Myth #7: You must Be in control of all thoughts to leverage your Law of Attraction

This is a demoralizing myth when you consider it, because it's impossible to regulate every thought. It doesn't require you to be able to watch every thought. In fact, there's no need to. All you have to do is be aware of your feelings.

Make use of your emotions to nourish positive thoughts and stifle negative thoughts. Your emotions are your guideline system, which can play a crucial role in harnessing the law of attraction. Thus, develop your abilities and select your thoughts with care. Understanding the thoughts that nourish and those that are not starts with analyzing the way you feel and determining the reason for your feeling. You can be able to distinguish the thoughts you have to pay attention to from ones you do not need as you control your mind effectively.

Step: Become a Decisive Creator. You'll be able to Get What You Want.

Myth 8 Law of Attraction Focuses on Shiny Pennies

Shiny pennies are a reference to glamorous items like bungalows, sports cars, plenty of cash, as well as other high-end things. Law of Attraction goes far more than just shiny pennies. Although you might appear the appearance of having these things however, it's the principle of attraction that is more than the material world, it's about memorable memories and joy. Attraction is all about what you feel right now and how you think about what you'll feel like after you've achieved your goals. It's all about feeling joy. A well-known quotation from Abraham is, "The standard of success in life doesn't depend on the things. It's not the amount of money you earn or the things you own. It's all about the amount of happiness that you experience." Many times, we desire certain things, thinking that they'll make us feel happy. Law of Attraction can be an easy way to experience the joy that you feel when you accomplish your objectives. Feel that feeling right now, the excitement of excitement, joy and happiness. amazing it feels to feel that you're helping the manifestation process.

Myth #9 the law of Attraction Only Works If the people around you believe in ItThis belief could be valid if your beliefs are based on in it because your thoughts shape your reality. However, you don't require anyone else to believe in the law in order to benefit from it. While it may be easier to have everyone else believe in it, the success of your business isn't dependent on it.

In addition, when you have increased your frequency then you are likely to draw attention to events, situations, and other people with similar energy. This means that if you're positive you'll attract positive people, rather than pessimistic ones. Don't use other people as an excuse to not create your ideal reality.

What is the time frame to get to get the Law of Attraction to Work?

Expectations of being received are greater in the twenty-first century than at any time in history. It's as if the current generation has lost its patience qualities. If you inquire there is a common belief that it can take a long time to obtain what you want. But, you can expect to receive satisfaction when your body and your mind are in sync in the field of cosmic harmony. I cannot emphasize this enough, but the vibrational frequency you create produces results that are in sync with yours. It is believed that the law of attraction usually is between 24 hours and 7 days to manifest minor events, from one or seven weeks to moderate manifestations, and anywhere between 6-months and 10 years for the most prominent manifestations. You can receive a response to your message within 24 hours. However, making a millionaire won't require longer that six months.

To find out what time the Law of Attraction can be effective for you, choose the size of the manifestation.

Small manifesto examples:

* Releasing a text or call from an ex-partner or friend
* Confirming an interview
* Confirming a date from your crush

Medium manifestation examples:

* Signifying a relationship
* Signifying a job promotion

* Signifying an the increase in the pay remuneration
* Manifesting weight loss

Large manifestation examples:
* Constructing a profitable business
* Constructing the family
* Promotion of job candidates to the CEO or higher

Other elements that affect the length of time law of attraction lasts are:

1. What Structures Your Thoughts Are

In the earlier chapters, your thoughts influence your life. It's one of the things that you have to accept. It will assist you understand why the manifestation process is taking so long. In general, your mind continuously is aware of what you do not have when you're looking for it. Let's say that you are seeking love. If you are spending a lot of time thinking about the length of time the process will take you're making it harder to achieve it. Law of Attraction is effective so give it time. It is just that we sometimes draw the incorrect things.

2. The level of attachment to the

Manifestation The Result

The amount of devotion you feel to the result affects the length of time that the law of attraction lasts. For instance, if you manifest a pair shoes that you don't really like, then you're fine with not having it.

In contrast, if you are concerned about having stability in your relationship, an increase in rank, or having the financial prosperity, it could appear a little complicated. Discover effective ways of letting loose of your attachment to these results, and the process may be less time-consuming.

3. Keep an eye out for signs

Although having a clear idea of what you want is important, keep alert for signs that the universe is satisfying your wishes. Don't be smug and you could be unable to see the signs. For instance, if are seeking love but you've rejected a number of dates because you are a pessimist You may have not noticed the warning signs. These signs may not be evident in the air; therefore it is important to be honest about them.

4. Faith in the Universe

The most basic rule to follow to follow in your law of attraction is to trust in the universe. Do not waste moment wondering if you're making your manifesting decisions right or worrying about what your desires. You should ask for what you need and believe to the Universe that it will provide.

5. The level of anxiety

When you feel stressed or worried because you've not manifested your desires in the right way it is actively removing it. Law of Attraction requires you to confront your fears and get rid of them and focus on positive thoughts.

Chapter 15: Health Attraction Mantra

Even even if you have one million dollars in your bank, all of it is to nothing if your don't have the vitality and health to utilize the funds. Do you realize that one of the things that is most in the way of optimism can be seen as health? The mind controls the body. If the brain has a positive outlook this energy will radiate to the body, too.

The secret to unlocking the Mantra of Health Attraction is to keep high-energy positive vibrations and an intense emotional state of mind about your goals and desires. It all starts with your beliefs and thinking.

Therefore, it is important to never ignore the positive effects of positive thinking to improve your well-being. Positive thinking can change your outlook on life, increasing your happiness levels throughout the day and accelerating your journey towards success. Positive thinking can bring benefits to your life. positive attitude can also affect the physical condition of your body in intriguing and unexpected ways.

Researchers continue to study the impact of positive thinking and optimism on well-being. It's not necessary to always smile however it is staying positive about what's going to be. It's as Suzanne Segerstrom, a professor of psychology at the University of Kentucky, puts it: "Happiness is an emotion that is an emotion. It is a belief regarding how the future will unfold."

Here are some benefits that Health Attraction Mantra can be able to have on your overall health:

1.) An increase in life span

Being able to live longer is something that we all want to be happy about. Positive outlooks can affect more than only your mood. Positive people tend to be more committed toward their goals. They more than successful in reaching their goals, are happier with their lives and enjoy greater physical and mental wellbeing in comparison to pessimistic people. Positive people are more likely to eat healthy food and exercise regularly and engage in preventative health.

Did You Know...

1.) A remarkable study of more than 600 hospitalized patients from Denmark discovered that those who had the best mood had a chance of being 60 percent higher likely to at least five years more..

2.) Researchers from the University of Pittsburgh School of Medicine examined data from over 100,000 women participating in an ongoing study which is funded by National Institutes of Health. Women who believed in optimism were 30% lower likely of heart disease than pessimists. Women who thought negatively are 23 percent less likely of cancer.

3.) A recent medical journal article revealed the connection between optimism and greater amounts of cholesterol that is good might result from this enthusiasm in a healthy lifestyle. The same hypothesis suggested that people who are optimistic suffer lower heart attacks and are about 9percent less likely to suffer stroke.

If you focus on the positive in your life and making it your goal to find a positive approach to issues by focusing on the positive, you can will live an enjoyable, long-lasting life.

2.) Positive Thinking Can Improve Your Immunity

Your thoughts can exert a significant influence upon your physical body. Immunity is one area in which your attitude and thoughts can be a significant influence.

Optimism doesn't just boost your mood. Have you ever considered that a glass half-full mental attitude can also boost your immune system? The fascinating research into the links between mental and physical health and well-being support the (initially confusing) belief that positive thoughts could boost your resistance to illness.

Have you heard that, in a study, researchers discovered that people who have positive outlooks are less susceptible to influenza and cold viruses. Additionally, they research suggests that those diagnosed with possibly fatal illnesses are more likely to experience noticeable and consistent improvement after treatment?

Positive thinkers who feel happier or more

positive about their goals and dreams are more resilient to immune. They are more likely to respond in more positive ways to stress, which allows them recover faster.

3.) Positive thinkers cope better When Experiencing Stress

Positive people are able to handle things better than people who are negative. They are able to focus more effectively in coming up with solutions rather than being distracted by negative influences. Additionally, the way people think has an effect in their overall health. So, If you are able to overcome negative thoughts, you'll be less likely to being affected by different illnesses. In addition you will also be able to handle any stress-related situation with enhanced concentration. This will help you relax and be more effective in dealing with stress.

Did you know that...

1.) People who have high stress levels are known for their increased blood pressure. Are they linked to a greater chance of developing health issues such as dementia and diabetes?

2.) A heart rate test on pessimists and

optimists reveal that people who are optimistic's bodies are able to return to a more relaxed state (including an average slowing of the heart) at a more rapid pace? 3) Women and men who reported being in a positive attitude (positive thought patterns) experienced lower amounts of cortisol, a stress hormone?

Chapter 16: Master Key System

After you have read the book. Here are what you need to know about the Master Key System that will allow you to transform your thoughts if you choose to to achieve this - and to connect with the source of real peace of mind.

You can print it and keep it somewhere you will see it frequently to act as a reminder to remember what you've learned so far.

1. There is nothing in this world that can't be most effectively achieved through a scientific knowledge of the ability of thinking.

2. The ability to think is shared by everyone. Man is because it is a thought process. Man's ability to think is unlimited, and therefore his creative capacity is endless.

3. We recognize that thought is creating for us the object we envision and brings it closer,

but we are unable to eliminate anxiety, fear or discontent and all of them are powerful thoughts, and constantly push the things we want further away. So that often it's one step forward , and two steps back.

4. Only way to stop from being regressed is to continue moving forward. Infinite vigilance is the price of success. It is a three-step process and each is vital. You need to first be armed with the understanding of your capabilities and courage to try; and finally and lastly, the conviction to act.

5. As a result, you can create an ideal business, a perfect home, the perfect group of family, and the perfect setting. There is no limit to materials or costs. Thought is all-powerful and is able to draw from the infinite pool of the primary substance for everything it needs. Infinite resources are thus available to you.

6. Your vision must be precise with a clear, concise, and clear definition and clear; having

an ideal for today and another tomorrow and the third one coming up next week, is to disperse your efforts and achieve nothing. Your end result will be an ineffective and chaotic mixture of wasted materials.

7. Undeterred. If a sculptor had started with a marble piece with a chisel in hand and altered his preferred method every 15 minutes, what results can he anticipate? What is the reason you should be expecting a different outcome when creating the most flexible of all materials that is the only substance you can truly call? Be sure to hold on to your goals and vision and stay with it.

8. As a result, any uncertainty or negative thoughts are usually result with the demise of wealth. The thought of independence that was supposed to require numerous years of hard work and work suddenly vanishes. It is usually discovered that property and money are not the only means of independence. Instead the only way to be independent is the ability to work with the power of thinking.

9. This working strategy can't be realized until you realize that the only ability you have is the ability to adapt your self to Divine and inexplicably enduring rules. It is impossible to alter the Infinite however, you can gain an knowledge about Natural laws. The result for this insight is the awareness of your capacity to align your thinking capabilities to match your Universal Thought, which is all-encompassing. Your capacity to cooperate to this Omnipotence will reveal the degree of success that you can meet.

10. The power of thought is a source of numerous counterfeits that can be fascinating or not however the outcomes are destructive instead of beneficial.

11. Of course, anxiety, fear or any negative thought result in the same results people who think that are of this type will eventually reap the fruits of what they've sown.

www.ingramcontent.com/pod-product-compliance
Lightning Source LLC
Chambersburg PA
CBHW071838080526
44589CB00012B/1039